Copyright and e-learning

a guide for practitioners

Jane Secker

facet publishing

Published by Facet Publishing
7 Ridgmount Street, London WC1E 7AE
www.facetpublishing.co.uk

Facet Publishing is wholly owned by CILIP: the Chartered Institute of
Library and Information Professionals.

British Library Cataloguing in Publication Data
A catalogue record for this book is available from the British Library.

ISBN 978-1-85604-665-7

First published 2010
Reprinted digitally thereafter

Text printed on FSC accredited material.

Mixed Sources
Product group from well-managed
forests and other controlled sources
www.fsc.org Cert no. SA-COC-1565
© 1996 Forest Stewardship Council

FSC

Typeset from author's files in 10/14 pt Linotype Palatino and Myriad
Pro by Facet Publishing Production.
Printed and made in Great Britain by MPG Books Group, UK.

In memory of
Ken Hayward and Herbert Cole

Contents

Acknowledgements

MANY THANKS TO the following people who helped with this book including Louise Le Bas and Helen Carley at Facet for encouraging and supporting me. Also special thanks to Maria Bell and June Hedges for their copyright knowledge and for reading early drafts. Thanks also to Steve Ryan, Kris Roger and Trevor Dawes.

Special thanks to Ned Potter from the University of Leeds for his help with the data analysis of the scanning survey presented in Chapter 2. Thanks also to David Crook from the Copyright Licensing Agency (CLA) for supplying data for this chapter.

I would also like to acknowledge the authors of the case studies which add valuable detail and real-life examples to this book including: June Hedges (University College London, UK), Monique Ritchie (Brunel University, UK), Mark Dilworth (Zurich International School, Switzerland), Upeksha Amarathunga and Ursula Loots (University of Auckland, New Zealand), Peter Robinson, Melissa Highton and Rowan Wilson (University of Oxford, UK).

The image on page 129 is reproduced with permission from the Joint Information Systems Committee (JISC)-funded Web2Rights project www.web2rights.org.uk (c) HEFCE, 2010.

I would also like to thank my employer the London School of Economics and Political Science (LSE) and my colleagues in the Centre for Learning Technology and Library who have always provided valuable advice and assistance.

Finally a big thank you to my husband Tim for his support while writing and for the endless cups of tea!

Jane Secker

Introduction

ATERIAL ON THE subjects of copyright and e-learning is essential
reading for those working in education today. Whether you are
a staff development officer, a teacher or an administrator, digital
technology and the internet will have impacted on the way in which you
work. This impact has been felt in both formal and informal learning in
school classrooms and staff development units, in almost all educational
establishments in the last ten years. Information and communication
technologies (ICTs) have offered teachers new ways of finding, creating
and distributing content to learners, extending the physical classroom to
include some form of digital space in which teachers can place resources.
Educational technologies provide learners with new ways of completing
their homework and of interacting with each other; students can discuss
ideas using online forums or can work together on projects using a
collaborative writing tool such as a wiki. The development of ICTs has
provided students with access to learning and resources at a time and place
convenient to them. Those working in student and staff support, in
libraries, IT, training and educational development have perhaps seen the
greatest changes, with the creation of new roles and responsibilities for e-
learning support. Increasingly both learners and teachers are working in
what is described as a new learning environment, a description that makes
reference to the digital or virtual space.

The classroom of the 21st century often has integral technology such as
interactive whiteboards with internet access, recording and lecture capture
tools. Our learners increasingly use technology in the classroom, bringing
with them laptops, mobile phones, digital cameras and recording devices,
leading them to have different expectations, skills and experience from
students of the past. Thus, as the teaching and learning environment
changes, so too does the way we teach. However, in this new and

exhilarating world of online teaching and learning, copyright is often an issue that is overlooked, perhaps until it is too late. Whereas online learning is seen as fun and exciting, copyright is usually seen as being boring and dull; it can be perceived as a barrier that stops teachers putting into practice their great ideas. For those charged with offering copyright advice, it can often seem as though they are the person inhibiting exciting new developments. It is also fair to say that if teachers do consider copyright issues, it is usually late in the day, meaning that any problems that occur are more difficult to resolve. Yet, with some foresight and understanding of the legislative framework in which education operates, copyright need not be a barrier to utilizing new technologies. If e-learning courses are designed with copyright in mind at the outset, it should not be a barrier to providing students with the information that they need in a timely and appropriate manner.

This book therefore aims to provide practical advice about a variety of copyright issues for those working in the broad field of online learning. The book seeks to dispel the belief that copyright is always a barrier to making materials available in e-learning environments, or that copyright laws are out of step with the ways in which modern teachers (and learners) wish to work. In recent years, in the UK, educational organizations such as Becta, HEFCE (Higher Education Funding Council for England) and JISC (Joint Information Systems Committee) have supported the publication of several guides in this area (see, for example, JISC, 2006; HEFCE, 2006) but there has been a distinct lack of monograph publications. This contrasts with the growth in publication of copyright guides written to support librarians, including Cornish (2009), Pedley (2007) and Norman (2004). This book aims to bridge this gap and provide a guide for practitioners working in the e-learning field. It is based on best practice developed by leading institutions that are supporting students in a blended learning environment and seven case studies of good practice are included. As e-learning support is extended from higher education (HE) to schools, colleges and other learning organizations, a good understanding of copyright and other intellectual property rights (IPR) issues is essential across the sector. This book will help staff to ensure that their e-learning initiatives are legal and that they do not expose the institution to the risk of legal challenges from publishers and other rights holders. It also provides a wealth of further reading and resources. However the book should not replace the legal advice that institutions are advised to seek if they are in any doubt over copyright issues.

Who should read this book?

The intended audience for this book is anyone working in education who uses some form of e-learning to support students. This includes both teachers and educational support staff such as learning technologists, librarians, educational developers, instructional designers and IT staff. It is aimed at the entire education sector from primary and secondary schools (known as K-12 in some countries) to higher education, although many examples do come from the higher education sector where copyright best practice is more developed. The book may also be relevant to those developing learning resources in the commercial sector, where e-learning is increasingly used for staff development. In the public sector, libraries, museums and archives and government departments are also using e-learning and so they too should find this book of interest. The book may also be helpful to those working in related areas, such as the health service, who are developing e-learning materials.

It is anticipated that the main audience for this book will be people living in the UK, although where possible an international perspective is included. While e-learning may mean that the geographical location of the teacher and learner are unimportant, copyright lawyers are concerned about where an educational establishment is based. Therefore, those providing e-learning support to international students need to carefully consider the copyright laws of the country where their institution is based. If materials are made available by a UK institution then usually copyright infringement would need to be pursued through courts in the UK. However, if material is being hosted outside of the UK then an awareness of the laws of other countries will be required. Furthermore, if a teacher moves from one country to another, for example from the United States to the UK, it is highly likely that familiarization with the law in the new country will be necessary. The author of this book is working in the UK and therefore the guidance provided is based on the laws of the United Kingdom. However, in recognition of differing copyright legislation around the world, international examples have been included where relevant; although examples come predominantly from the English-speaking world including the United States, Canada, New Zealand and Australia. The book recognizes that many of the changes in UK copyright law are being led by attempts to harmonize copyright legislation across the EU (European Union). However, with the exception of Ireland, other European countries are not considered in any detail.

Finally, this book is intended as a best practice guide, and should not be considered legal advice. The author is not a lawyer and has deliberately written this book as a guide for practitioners, rather than for lawyers or copyright experts. There are some references to legislation and case law, but other books cover these topics in far greater detail. In addition, educational establishments are advised to seek legal advice on problematic copyright issues and to develop rigorous internal intellectual property rights policies.

Overview of the content

Chapter 1 provides an overview of copyright and other intellectual property rights as they relate to e-learning in several English-speaking countries. It also provides background information about the development of e-learning, and its relationship to both face-to-face teaching and distance education. This chapter explores how the digital environment differs from the classroom and considers issues such as copying for educational purposes and what the law permits. Finally it provides details about new developments in copyright such as the open access and Creative Commons movements. The case study comes from Brunel University who have appointed a Copyright and Digital Resources Officer to tackle these and other issues.

Chapter 2 considers how to reuse published content in e-learning. It will look specifically at the situation in the UK where the Copyright Licensing Agency licences permit materials to be digitized for education. Results from a recent survey into scanning activity in higher education are presented, demonstrating the concern that exists amongst higher education librarians to educate staff about copyright issues. The chapter also briefly considers the situation in other countries, specifically the United States and the digitization of archival or other unpublished works and the associated copyright issues. Two case studies are included in this chapter, one from UCL (University College London) examining scanning and copyright services provided by their Library, and one examining electronic reserves in the United States.

Chapter 3 looks specifically at multimedia content and how this might be used in e-learning; it considers, for example, the digitization of off-air recordings under the Educational Recording Agency (ERA) Licence. It also explores the increasing use of lecture capture and the copyright and IPR issues that are raised by this procedure. It considers podcasting and provides a useful list of multimedia and image collections available to the education community. The case study is concerned with podcasting using iTunes at the University of Oxford.

Chapter 4 looks at 'born digital' resources and outlines the copyright issues concerned with each of these in turn. Increasingly, embedded in born digital content are a variety of digital rights management (DRM) procedures designed to protect the content from being reused. This chapter covers specific concerns that need to be addressed when using different types of digital resources, including external websites, and looks at implicit and explicit licences for electronic resources and websites. It includes a case study from the University of Auckland examining the Electronic Course Materials service provided by their Library.

The digital environment is changing rapidly and Chapter 5 examines new and emerging technologies, sometimes known as Web 2.0 technologies, and their associated copyright issues. The chapter provides an overview of these technologies and the changing digital environment. It then considers issues such as relying on third-party hosted materials, where copyright lies in works with multiple creators or if individuals contribute to Web 2.0 services. The chapter provides examples of how several Web 2.0 sites handle copyright in terms of protecting their own rights and handling others uploading content to their sites or reusing material. Examples from some of the most popular sites such as Flickr, Facebook and Wikipedia are included. The chapter includes a case study from Zurich International School examining how students are encouraged to use emerging technologies in a responsible way that respects copyright law.

Finally Chapter 6 explains how to devise a copyright training programme for staff in an educational establishment. It considers issues such as who should deliver the programme and the support that they will require, the intended audience and differing approaches you might need

– for example, for training academic staff in comparison to administrative staff. Methods of delivery are considered, including the need for face-to-face sessions, utilization of the web and the role of booklets, guides and leaflets. Finally this chapter considers how to deal with copyright queries and provides sources of further advice and support. It includes a case study from the London School of Economics and Political Science that explains how a copyright training programme has been devised and rolled out to staff across the institution.

One of the strengths of this book is that it includes case studies from several high profile UK universities, and also from educational establishments in the USA, New Zealand and Europe. The case studies explore issues raised in each chapter in more detail and provide specific examples of best practice. They are:

♦ Case Study 1: The Copyright and Digital Resources Officer at Brunel University, UK
♦ Case Study 2: UCL library services' course reading service, UK
♦ Case Study 3: Electronic reserves and copyright in a US university
♦ Case Study 4: Open educational resources, Oxford on iTunes U and OpenSpires, University of Oxford, UK
♦ Case Study 5: The Electronic Course Material service of the University of Auckland Library, New Zealand
♦ Case Study 6: Zurich International School – e-learning and copyright
♦ Case Study 7: Developing a copyright training programme for staff at LSE, UK.

Throughout this book the author assumes that readers have no previous knowledge of UK copyright law or the issues relating to copyright and e-learning. References are included at the end of each chapter and suggested further reading is included in the Conclusion to the book. A Glossary is also provided at the end of the book, which explains technical terms and acronyms (although these are spelt out in the main text on the first occasion of their use). Wherever possible the author has tried to avoid legal jargon.

Definitions

Before proceeding any further it would be helpful, to provide context and understanding, to define some of the terms that are used throughout this book. The author is based in the UK higher education sector and a familiarity with the terminology used in this field is apparent in the text. If you are new to any of the acronyms then it is suggested that you refer to the Glossary.

E-learning

E-learning – 'electronic learning,'or 'online learning' at its broadest level – is defined as the use of computer technology to support teaching and learning. However, this definition suggests that simply using a computer in any part of learning, for example in order to word-process an essay, might be e-learning and this is not the case. A more accurate definition of e-learning is that it is the use of computer technology as an integral part of the learning process. In most instances some form of e-learning system or platform is used. These are sometimes called virtual learning environments (VLEs), course management systems (CMS) or learning management systems (LMS). The term VLE is used throughout this book to refer to what some might call a CMS or LMS. An e-learning platform provides a secure online space where resources and activities are available to the student. Password protection is almost always in place, so that placing material on a VLE means that it is restricted to students and staff in the institution. In some instances e-learning may be replacing some of the face-to-face or classroom-based activities, such as a lecture or a seminar. However, in many instances the online resources and activities complement face-to-face teaching. There are increasing numbers of institutions, particularly in higher education or in the field of continuing professional development (CPD), which now offer distance learning courses delivered completely using e-learning. This means students do not need to attend the institution in person but can carry out their learning at a time and place of their choice. It should be recognized that the term 'e-learning' includes a broad spectrum of models of education.

E-learning platforms

E-learning platforms, such as VLEs, are used by the majority of higher and further educational institutions in the UK today. In the schools sector VLEs are becoming increasingly common and are often implemented and supported by the local education authority.

Commercial proprietary systems and open-source solutions are used in equal numbers in higher, further and school level education. In the commercial and health areas e-learning can be supported by a dedicated platform, a system such as SharePoint, or through using an intranet. E-learning is used for formal education, informal learning and also for continuing professional development and staff development activities. In many cases, some form of face-to-face training also complements the online support. In general e-learning platforms are password protected so although material is placed on a network, it is not made available on the internet to a wider audience.

Blended learning

Blended learning is a related term, used to describe a blend of the face-to-face and online learning. True e-learning is in fact fairly rare and many institutions will provide online support to complement their face-to-face teaching. In a 'blended learning' situation students usually attend traditional lectures or seminars but have access to a variety of online resources. They may undertake online assessments and use discussion forums, but they will not be distance learning students. This mode of education is highly flexible, allowing students to catch up if they miss classes. It is increasingly common in higher education where many students will work part-time to help fund their studies. It also allows students to live some distance from the university campus.

Copyright and intellectual property rights

Copyright is a subset of a broader set of intellectual property rights which give exclusive rights to the owner of a work. Related IPRs include patents, trademarks, designs and databases rights. These are not discussed in any detail in this book, which concentrates on copyright. Copyright coverage is extensive, covering written materials (known as literary works), artistic, dramatic and musical works, works of architecture, sound recordings, film and video, photographs, and websites. Copyright laws exist throughout the world and international copyright agreements such as the Berne

Convention (1886) mean that there is automatic protection against the copying and selling of works beyond their country of origin. The laws often date back to the early days of publishing, yet in most countries the law has tried to reflect the emergence of new technologies. Copyright laws do not cover ideas in themselves; in many countries to qualify for copyright protection the expression of ideas needs to be 'fixed' in some way, for example in written or recorded format.

Born digital content and digitization

Another important concept central to this book is that of 'born digital' content, a notion which separates content *created* in digital format from that which is digitized from a print or analogue source. Born digital content is discussed in greater detail in Chapter 4, including the variety of appropriate file formats.

Jane Secker

1

E-learning and copyright: background

Introduction

This chapter considers copyright and the digital environment in some detail. It provides an overview of the major differences between copyright laws in several English-speaking countries in the world and how they apply to e-learning. The focus of this book is on the UK, but copyright laws in countries such as the United States, Australia, Canada and New Zealand are explored. It does not provide legal advice for those working in e-learning but examines how copying can be undertaken for educational purposes. This includes what copying is permitted under exceptions in the law and how copyright issues impact on face-to-face teaching. The chapter also defines e-learning more specifically and looks at the 'new learning environment' which includes the use of the internet, intranets and secure networks such as virtual learning environments, course management systems and other online teaching environments. This chapter considers how the digital environment differs from the face-to-face learning environment of the classroom. It also explores new developments in scholarly publishing including the open access movement and open-source software along with the development of what some see as an alternative to copyright – the Creative Commons movement. This chapter includes the first case study, which is from Brunel University, where the institution took the decision to appoint a Copyright and Digital Resources Officer in light of the copyright challenges they were facing.

Recognizing the copyright dilemma

Much of what teachers wish to do in an online learning environment is no different to what they have done previously in the classroom. Students are given set reading to undertake, asked to critique a work of art or consult a manuscript source. They may work individually or in groups. The difference lies in how students might access learning resources, which are often copyright-protected materials. Technology offers the teacher the possibility of providing students with a perfect copy of a copyright work such as an e-book, a music file or a piece of digital video. Early digital library research projects, such as those funded by the JISC in the 1990s as part of the eLib programme, recognized the complex copyright issues that the digitization process could cause. The background to this programme is discussed in greater detail by other authors (Rusbridge, 1998; Secker, 2004), being outside of the scope of this book. Nevertheless, many early digitization projects in libraries throughout the world deliberately concentrated on using material that was out of copyright, thus avoiding the need to process copyright permissions, which are both time-consuming and potentially problematic if the owner of a work cannot be traced. However, in the UK, JISC launched several projects as part of eLib to tackle this issue head on looking at on-demand publishing and electronic short loan. These various projects ultimately led to the establishment of HERON (Higher Education Resources ON-demand) funded initially by JISC as a project. HERON subsequently became a commercial service providing digitization and copyright services to higher education in the UK and more widely. This is discussed in greater detail in Chapter 2.

Through early projects in e-learning and digital libraries, JISC became increasingly aware of the legal ramifications of working in a digital environment. Consequently the JISC Legal service was launched in 2000 to provide advice and support on a wide range of legal issues for the further and higher education community. The JISC Legal website (www.jisclegal.ac.uk) provides a wealth of legal advice and guidance over the use of ICTs in education, including copyright issues. In recent years many JISC-funded projects involving digital resources have mentioned copyright or IPR issues in their final report. JISC have numerous resources and tools available on their website and a selection of these are listed in the Conclusion to this book.

The development of e-learning

Before considering copyright issues any further, this next section will briefly provide an overview of e-learning support. A list of general readings on this topic is provided in the Conclusion of the book. However, e-learning has become increasingly important in education and training, with the proliferation of digital technologies and the widespread availability of network infrastructure, which facilitate high speed broadband capability. In higher education e-learning has had the greatest impact, with significant investment from funding bodies such as JISC, who have provided the infrastructure, through the JANET network and research and development funding for projects and initiatives. This means that every higher education institution (HEI) in the UK has invested significantly in digital technologies to support teaching and learning. Student's classroom learning is primarily supported through the use of VLEs, with the commercial system Blackboard and the open-source system Moodle, dominating the field.

In the further education sector most colleges also now have VLEs, with the most common platform being the open-source system Moodle. Essentially what these systems provide is a relatively easy to use platform to distribute content to learners, with built-in educational tools or activities to engage learners and to facilitate learning, such as discussion tools, assessment tools, file upload and collaborative workspaces. In fairness, true e-learning, as defined in the Introduction, is rare, but most educational establishments have recognized that providing online support for learners, in addition to face-to-face teaching, offers many rewards for both the teacher and the learner. The use of e-learning is largely linked to the need to provide students in higher and further education with greater flexibility, in terms of the time and place in which they do their learning. Funding cuts have meant that there are now far higher numbers of part-time students and students who need to work while studying. This means that students increasingly need the support provided by electronic access.

Meanwhile, in the schools sector e-learning has been slower to develop, but progressed more rapidly following recent investment from central government through Becta (www.becta.org.uk). Becta's role is 'to ensure that technology is used at its best in the British education system' (Becta, 2009a). They have run several events and produced numerous resources to help encourage the effective use of e-learning. Developments in the schools sector were largely driven by the UK government's e-Strategy (DfES, 2005) launched in 2005 that sought to provide a 'cradle to grave' approach to using technology in learning. The e-Strategy also set the expectations that:

◆ by spring 2008 every pupil should have access to a personalized online learning space with the potential to support an e-portfolio (provided by their local authority)
◆ by 2010 every school should have integrated learning and management systems (a comprehensive suite of learning platform technologies) (Becta, 2009b).

Often known as 'learning platforms' in schools, VLEs are becoming common place along with the use of other classroom technologies such as interactive whiteboards.

Blended learning

Many HEIs invested in e-learning solutions drawn by the lure of supporting students at a distance. Distance learning is seen as a useful way of expanding student numbers without the need for additional teaching space. It also meets the growing demand for education throughout the globe. However, the financial investment associated with distance education is not insignificant. The UK witnessed the financial collapse of the much heralded 'e-University' in 2005 at a reported cost of over £500 million. This led many institutions to reconsider how they might use e-learning and focus on what is often called 'blended learning'. This is defined in the Introduction as the support of on-campus face-to-face students with an e-learning platform that enables them to access lecture materials, resources and readings and communicate with their peers and tutors outside of the classroom. This model has become increasingly common as higher education has expanded and the profile of students has changed. Since 1992, the UK and many other English-speaking countries have seen a significant expansion in higher education. Participation levels in HE in the UK are now approximately 50%. With increasingly large class sizes and more students studying while working part- (or even full-) time, e-learning, or blended learning, opens up higher education and provides students with flexibility to learn at a time and place convenient to them. Thus, it has been linked to the widening participation agenda in the UK, which sees students from non-traditional backgrounds entering universities. Here, student retention can be a key issue and many e-learning systems include administrative functions that allow student participation to be tracked to alert tutors to potential problems early on.

E-learning and digital resources

While many e-learning researchers have long advocated that VLEs should be interactive environments, where students complete tasks and activities rather than simply access content, it is fair to say that many teachers are lured into using VLEs or course management systems as a document repository. Materials such as PowerPoint presentations, lecture notes and essential readings seem to be the obvious contenders for uploading onto the learning platform. A typical course in any HEI will inevitably become an electronic file store for materials, which previously were included in course handbooks or given out in the classroom. In recent years institutions are also starting to invest in lecture capture systems, so not only can slides from a presentation be accessed, but also a recording of the lecture alongside presentation slides will be available. Podcasts, screen capture and other video and audio production are becoming increasingly sophisticated. Consequently many e-learning support teams now work alongside more traditional audiovisual technicians in providing services in this area as the technology improves and the costs are reduced. Bandwidth was until recently an issue with audio and video material in digital format, due to the large file sizes of the materials, but streaming servers now allow this content to be delivered over networks.

The wide availability of digital resources, be they useful web-based resources, e-journals or e-books leads many teachers to try to include as many learning resources as possible within the VLE for the convenience of their students. Librarians are aware that students and academic staff visit the library building less frequently, as many prefer the convenience of desktop access from their office or home that authentication systems allow. It is therefore no surprise that teachers who use the VLE want to include direct links to access full text materials, for example from the course reading list. Many teachers are unaware of the complex licensing arrangements negotiated by libraries that allow them to access resources such as e-journals and e-books. In fact with more sophisticated authentication procedures, many teachers are not aware when they are using a subscription resource as opposed to content freely available on the internet. The desire to provide students with as many resources as possible to help their learning can inevitably lead to copyright issues. Teachers will argue that they are simply trying to help students get access to material, however the ease with which content can be downloaded from the internet or a library database or even scanned from hardcopy, means it is all too easy to break licence agreement terms and conditions or infringe another's copyright. The general perception that there exists some sort of blanket exception for educational or not-for-profit use prevails in education, particularly outside of higher education (which is better resourced and consequently more likely to employ copyright experts to advise staff and students). Additionally many teachers believe that because they are distributing content to students via a secure network this differs from making material available on the internet.

Our learners: 'the Google Generation'?

Before turning to copyright laws, it is also worth briefly mentioning the recent research that has looked at the characteristics of students today. Many recent reports (Rowlands et al., 2008; RIN (Research Information Network, 2007) have suggested that young people have a different relationship to technology than earlier generations. Various authors have labelled them as 'the Net Generation', 'the Google Generation', 'Generation Y' or 'digital natives'. While it is true to say that in much of the developed world many young people have greater access to technology, be it the internet, mobile phones, video games or MP3 players, perhaps more worryingly, there is also some evidence to suggest that young people have a different (or lack of) understanding of copyright laws. Rowlands et al. (2008, 301) qualified the findings from earlier research that suggested that young people did not respect intellectual property, saying they found this only to be partly true, while stating: 'Young people feel that copyright regimes are unfair and unjust and a big age gap is opening up. The implications for libraries and for the information industry of a collapse of respect for copyright are potentially very serious.'

Certainly what is clear is that students tend to expect resources to be freely available to them, either on the internet or in their online learning environment. Moreover, students perhaps more than staff have a limited understanding of why copyright might present those delivering or supporting their teaching with difficulties.

Brief introduction to UK copyright law

These next sections will go on to explore copyright in greater detail, including why the laws exist and what they permit in terms of copyright for educational purposes in the UK, and contrasting the situation with some other countries in the world.

Copyright laws were intended to protect the creative industries and to ensure that intellectual and financial rewards for investments were returned to their rightful owners. Many countries talk about the need for balance in terms of adequate copyright protection against theft and piracy, versus generous educational provisions that foster the free flow of ideas. In the UK, copyright does not require a registration process and provided that works meet certain criteria, then they qualify for automatic copyright protection upon their creation. These criteria state that the work must be:

◆ original
◆ fixed or recorded in some form
◆ created by a qualified national.

Usually the primary author owns the copyright to a work, but this is dependent upon the nature of the work (see Table 1.1). In the case of literary works such as books, authors are often fairly clear, but identifying the owner of copyright for works such as films and sound recordings can become more complex. So for example in the case of sounding recordings the author of the work is the producer and the company who made the recording owns copyright. However, if a sound recording is performed it qualifies for performance rights. In the case of films the producer and the principal director are the author of the work. Cornish (2009, 12) provides an excellent overview of the issues surrounding copyright ownership if you are in any doubt. Don't forget that as a property right, copyright can also be bought, sold and transferred to another. In many cases the

Table 1.1 *UK law on duration of copyright by type of material (Copyright, Designs and Patents Act 1988, OPSI, 2009)*

Type of material	Duration of copyright
Literary and artistic works	70 years from the death of the author
Dramatic and musical works	70 years from publication if no named author
Sound recordings	50 years from the date of recording
Films	50 years following the last to die of: the principal director, producer, author of screenplay, composer of soundtrack
Broadcasts	50 years from the date of broadcast
Typographical layout	25 years from publication
Unpublished works	70 years from the death of the author
Crown copyright	125 years from publication but subject to a waiver

copyright owner of a work can be identified from the universal copyright symbol placed somewhere prominently on the work (for example, © Jane Secker 2009), however its use is not a prerequisite for copyright protection in the UK or for much of the world.

Cornish (2009, 39–43) provides greater detail about the duration of copyright and should be consulted for specific queries such as protection for authors from outside of the European Economic Area (EEA) and protection for works with multiple authors. In terms of Crown Copyright material, generally this can be copied as it is subject to a waiver that allows unrestricted copying of the material as part of the public right to information about government. In addition, most US government materials are also not covered by copyright and unrestricted copying is permitted. For further details of international copyright agreements such as the Berne Convention, that award protection to materials around the world, the UK's Intellectual Property Office provides an excellent overview (Intellectual Property Office, 2008).

'Fair dealing'

UK law (and many copyright laws throughout the world) have a provision known as 'fair dealing' which many confuse with educational copying permitted under the law. Fair dealing is in fact a defence that could be used in court rather than a right under law and it states that a single copy of literary, dramatic, musical or artistic work can be made for the following specific purposes:

♦ private non-commercial study and research
♦ criticism and review
♦ the reporting of news
♦ government administration.

Much photocopying and scanning of published works undertaken in an educational context falls under the fair dealing provision; for example, single copies made by teachers for their research or by students as part of their private study. However, distribution of copies via an e-learning platform constitutes multiple copying and thus cannot be considered as fair dealing. In addition, fair dealing in the UK does not currently extend to films, sound recordings or broadcasts, or to electronic resources.

Educational copying and the law

Provisions for educational copying are enshrined in almost all copyright laws throughout the world, but with many caveats. For example, in the UK, sections 32 to 36 of the Copyright, Designs and Patents Act 1988 includes an exception that permits copying for educational purposes. However, copyright exceptions have a problematic relationship with technology, even it would seem the humble photocopier. UK law is clear that copying for educational purposes is permitted, provided a *reprographic process* is not used. Therefore, it is no real surprise that the widespread availability of scanners has caused problems to copyright legislators across the globe. The high cost and size of photocopiers historically meant that the chance of regular households having such a machine was slim and, in addition, copies made from photocopiers were clearly degraded in terms of quality when compared to the original work. However, the inexpensive desktop scanner that many people now own in their homes can create digital copies of protected works quickly and efficiently and to a high standard. Yet without permission these copies are rarely suitable for use in teaching. Moreover, copying existing digital content, such as a portable document format (PDF) file, is even simpler and leads to no degradation of quality from the original file.

Since the advent of the internet it is interesting to trace how different countries have dealt with educational copying in terms of making material available via a learning platform. Whilst not attempting to be comprehensive, the following section includes details from a selection of English-speaking countries. It aims to highlight how technology is causing governments around the world to reconsider their copyright laws and try to bring them up to date. Yet the pressure to amend the laws seems to often be coming from commercial concerns, particularly industries such as the music and film industries that are attempting to combat internet piracy and illegal file-sharing. In trying to clamp down on this type of copying, legislators could well be causing even further problems for educators who simply want to allow students and researchers to be able to access information in the most convenient format. The measures that are in place in many countries are already overly burdensome for administrators and librarians. One hopes that in the future the needs of education can be balanced fairly against the need for copyright owners to receive just rewards for their endeavours, and that this will be recognized by governments around the world as they undertake copyright reforms.

Copyright and educational copying in the UK

Copyright is an exclusive right given to the primary author or creator of a work. Not everything is covered by copyright but in the UK as in most other countries, protection is given to a variety of original material that is fixed in some form. Therefore copyright can protect a broadcast, a recording or a literary or artistic work, but it cannot be used to protect an idea – it fundamentally protects the expression of an idea. This book is not a comprehensive guide for librarians to copying under the law, as several other authors have already produced comprehensive and up-to-date books on this topic. See the further reading at the end of the book, but notable authors who have produced invaluable guides for UK librarians or archivists include Norman (2004), Pedley (2007, 2008) and Cornish (2009). Both the work of Norman and Cornish are useful supplements to this book as they are set out as questions and answers to common copyright dilemmas that those dealing with copyright queries are frequently asked. Meanwhile Pedley's *Digital Copyright* (2007) is particularly useful for those interested in relevant case law in this area. This work seeks neither to replace nor replicate these existing publications, but rather to provide a focus on how copyright issues impact on e-learning.

This section serves as an introduction to the legal framework in which practitioners operate. It will compare how copying for e-learning can be undertaken within the law in the UK, and then contrast this with several countries including Ireland, the United States of America, Australia, Canada and New Zealand. By way of interest, the law in terms of educational copying in Ireland is also briefly discussed but for practical reasons this book cannot provide a comprehensive overview of the legal position across the globe. Therefore, the focus is deliberately on the major English-speaking countries in the world to provide advice for e-learning practitioners. There are also other books available which include much more detailed copyright advice for respective countries. These are referenced in the Conclusion and should be consulted for specific advice pertaining to a country outside of the UK. Copyright legislation in the former Commonwealth countries (including Canada, Australia and New Zealand) is based on UK law and so is broadly similar. The key differences in terms of educational copying are discussed in the next section. In the USA, the law differs for the 1976 Copyright Act includes the concept of 'fair use' 'Fair use' is generally seen as a more permissive approach to copyright for it permits copyright material to be copied for educational use. Significantly in the UK and many other countries, much educational or classroom copying needs to be undertaken under a licence from the respective reprographic rights body, as UK law does not include the 'fair use' concept.

An important query often raised by teachers who are developing content to be delivered throughout the world concerns the jurisdiction that applies when they are copying material. Does the law of the country in which they work take precedence over the law of the country where the content will be delivered? The answer put simply is that if you are developing an e-learning course in a UK institution then the laws of the UK apply (or if you are developing a course in a US educational institution then US law applies), even if students from a different country might be accessing this material. This query really only arises in the higher education sector where many traditional campus universities now utilize e-learning to deliver distance learning courses across the world.

Distance or open learning higher education developed as early as the 19th century in the UK and has always been popular in the US and Australia where distance might prevent people from attending a university in person. The development of robust e-learning platforms has meant that even traditional campus-based universities can deliver some of their courses as distance education. In the past, distance education was a specialist mode of delivery that was usually delivered by specialist units or institutions such as the Open University. Knowledge of copyright issues is a prerequisite and distance education universities, such as the Open University in the UK, have a rights and permissions department to negotiate contracts and clear content for use. However, many HEIs have recently ventured into the realm of distance education and do not have specialist staff involved in this work. This means that there is rarely any detailed understanding of the potential copyright issues associated with this form of delivery. Consequently, getting answers to fundamental questions, such as the jurisdiction that applies in terms of copying material or protecting that material, can all too easily necessitate the institution needing to seek expensive legal advice.

In general there are a number of ways that copying works can be undertaken without infringing copyright laws. These include:

- copying small amounts of a work (copyright protects a substantial part of a work although no definition of what 'substantial' might be is provided in UK law and it does not relate simply to quantity)
- copying material where copyright has expired. Copyright protection is limited in terms of duration and a summary is listed in Table 1.1 (thus unrestricted copying of a work which is out of copyright and in the 'public domain' is permitted)
- copying material under a statutory exception; for instance, copying under 'fair dealing' in the UK for the purposes of criticism and review
- copying material under a licence which extends the limits provided under law – for example the Copyright Licensing Agency offer licences for the education sector to permit multiple copying of published works with limits
- copying material with permission from the copyright owner.

Copyright and e-learning in the UK

Under UK law copying for an educational purpose is limited. Although the Copyright, Designs and Patents Act 1988 (hereafter known as 'the Act') makes a provision for educational copying under Sections 32 to 36, the Act does not permit copying by a reprographic process. In practice this means that photocopying, scanning or copying a work using digital technology for education is prohibited. The technology that can be used to make copies is not specified in the Act. The only reference to how copies are delivered came in 2003 when the UK law was amended by The Copyright and Related Rights Regulations (Statutory Instrument No. 2498) which:

◆ redefined broadcasts to specifically exclude internet transmission (or podcasts)
◆ gave copyright holders the exclusive right to 'communicate a work to the public'
◆ defined this right as making the material available by 'electronic transmission', that is, via the internet and/or broadcasting the work.

(OPSI, 2003)

Prior to this amendment it was technically illegal to view websites, as doing so created temporary copies on the viewer's computer. However this amendment stated that copyright is not infringed by:

the making of a temporary copy which is transient or incidental, which is an integral and essential part of a technological process and the sole purpose of which is to enable:

(a) a transmission of the work in a network between third parties by an intermediary; or
(b) a lawful use of the work.

(OPSI, 2003)

There are some notable exceptions to copyright; for example, under 'fair dealing', students in education are permitted to make single copies of copyright works for private non-commercial research or study. Similarly,

Section 32(3) permits copying for 'the purposes of an examination by way of setting the questions, communicating the questions to the candidates or answering the questions' (OPSI, 2009). Many agree that the examination definition also covers student theses, so that they can include copyright material, although if they are subsequently published this will require permission. Section 36 covers reprographic copying by educational establishments, stating that 1% of a work can be copied in any quarter of the year, but it goes on to state that where a licence is available this should regulate copying. Licences are available for the education sector, therefore universities, schools and colleges would be unwise to rely on Section 36 to digitize copyright material for e-learning.

Section 36 of the act means that multiple copying of copyright works either for the classroom or for e-learning is largely undertaken in the UK under licence from the reprographic rights organization, the Copyright Licensing Agency. Since 1999 the CLA have offered a digitization licence to the higher education sector. Initially this was a transactional licence that meant copies had to be paid for on a per page per student basis. In 2005 the first blanket licence for the higher education community was issued by the CLA. This licence operated for three years as an optional addition to the institutional photocopying licence. In 2008, the first comprehensive photocopying, scanning and digital licence was issued and take up by universities has been extremely high. It has led to the vast expansion of scanning services in HE libraries to support the parallel growth in e-learning. The use of this licence is discussed in greater detail in Chapter 2. However, the CLA also offer licences for other sectors, including further education, schools, businesses and the health sector.

Visually impaired persons (VIPs) and students with disabilities

A further piece of copyright legislation that impacts on education is the Copyright (Visually Impaired Persons) Act 2002 (OPSI, 2002). This allows single copies of copyright works (literary, dramatic, musical or artistic work or a published edition) to be made for VIPs for accessibility purposes if it is not available commercially. The copy needs to include a statement to say that it has been made under this provision and needs to include a sufficient acknowledgement. Educational establishments or not-for-profit organizations (NPOs) are also permitted to make multiple copies for VIPs.

The Gowers Review

While the UK copyright act has been modified many times since 1988 using statutory instruments, in December 2005 HM Treasury launched a widespread review of UK intellectual property rights law. The Treasury launched this review as IPR issues were seen as central to supporting the UK economy. The recommendations made by the Gowers Report (HM Treasury, 2006) were widely criticized by those in higher education as not going far enough to recognize the pace of technological change. They have yet to be implemented in UK law but in summary include:

◆ a specific provision for distance learning
◆ clarification over copying items where copyright cannot be traced (orphan works)
◆ clarification over format shifting for preservation purposes particularly of multimedia works.

The Gowers Review sought to address intellectual property issues that had arisen largely due to developments in new technology. Gowers aimed to provide a balance, but its reception in the education community has been lukewarm, with many seeing the review as not going far enough, in particular in terms of fair dealing. To date the UK government has not implemented the recommendations. The issue of 'orphan works', that is items where copyright ownership is difficult or impossible to trace, has caused many problems in academic institutions. Orphan works consume a considerable amount of staff time in attempts to track down rights holders to obtain permission to copy the materials. On occasions where the rights cannot be traced, an institution needs to assess on a case-by-case basis the risks involved if the material is copied without permission. Institutions also need to maintain records to demonstrate that all possible avenues were explored.

There has also been widespread concern that copyright law is being undermined by contract law, particularly in terms of the licensing of electronic resources, where the terms of a licence are more restrictive than the law permits. In terms of copyright and preservation, it had been hoped that Gowers might address the issue of format shifting for preservation or access purposes. However the UK is lagging behind other countries where currently only single copies can be made of literary works and sound and video collections are not covered by the fair dealing clause. Responses to Gowers were received from bodies such as the Society of College, National and University Libraries (SCONUL), Universities UK (UUK) and several universities. One institution that had a particular interest in the review was the Open University (OU), which called on the government to dispense with the distinction between e-learning and distance learning. The former Head of Intellectual Property at the OU, Richard McCracken (2007) argued that copyright legislation should focus on purpose and use rather than media and location. Macracken also suggested that the definition of the classroom should be extended to include the electronic classroom. In a recent meeting between the UK government and the Libraries and Archives Copyright Alliance (LACA), the SCONUL Secretary Toby Bainton called on Secretary of State David Lammy to consider the 'excessive bureaucracy' that is placed on UK libraries to administer licences and the inconsistencies in the copyright legislation (SCONUL, 2009).

igital Economy Act 2010

nother legislative change of significance to the e-learning community is the UK's Digital Economy Act [HL 2009–10] which became law in April 2010. At the time of writing, the impact of the Act on education was unclear. The Act followed the Digital Britain White Paper (DCMS, 2009) that addressed the UK's strategy for implementing a digital economy and infrastructure. The White Paper identified a number of problems with current copyright law and it was hoped the Act might address, among other issues, the copying of 'orphan works' and images from the internet. Amendments to the Act along these lines were withdrawn as it was rushed through Parliament in the run up to the general election. Clauses 4-18 are of particular relevance to education and deal with the issue of online copyright infringement. Persons found guilty of infringement can have their internet access blocked and internet service providers (ISPs) can be fined by Ofcom for failing to act against persistent offenders. Critics fear that this legislation will serve the interests of the film and music industries who wish to crack down on illegal file sharing. *The Guardian* (2009) recently argued that the Act:

will force internet service providers to become copyright police, obliging them to provide lists of violations to copyright owners. . . . All this will drive up the costs of web access, by piling duties on providers. Add the more defensible surcharges to pay for next generation services, and Digital Britain risks becoming a land beset by an even deeper digital divide.

Case Study 1: The Copyright and Digital Resources Officer at Brunel University, UK

Monique Ritchie

Introduction

In 2004/05, Brunel University Library created a new dedicated post to manage copyright in the academic environment, with a focus on digital copyright: the Copyright and Digital Resources Officer. Like most educational institutions, recent changes to copyright law and licensing schemes, and the increased use of e-learning environments and e-resources, threw copyright to the forefront of strategic planning. There was a strong recognition among Library and senior University management that the digital age posed particular challenges at a time when the University's e-learning strategy was evolving rapidly.

Copyright management was not new to Brunel, but with the implementation of the EU Copyright Directive into UK legislation in 2003, there was a rapid evolution from a role that the University was previously able to adequately manage by sharing the responsibilities for licence administration and copyright advice within the existing staff infrastructure. It became increasingly apparent that the existing provisions were no longer adequate when faced with an increasingly intricate licensing and legislative framework.

Before the post was filled, it became clear that a University-wide copyright consultancy service was required, with the Learning and Teaching Development Unit (responsible for e-learning), and Computing and Media Services in particular, lending their weight to support the Library's bid to create the new post.

Remit, scope and position in the institution

The remit is broad, with the Copyright Officer responsible for providing support on copyright and IPR issues to all staff and students, academic and non-academic. However, the post sits within the Library staff structure, as, despite the close links with external departments and Schools, key stakeholders are primarily engaged in teaching, learning and research functions. The Library naturally occupies a central position in relation to these, and is quite often the first port of call for questions – library or non-library related.

Initially, the post was managed directly by the Director of Library Services, who oversaw the direction and focus of the role in the early stages, particularly as it had linkages with the University's strategic planning process. In August 2008, the Library underwent a restructuring process to ensure that roles best met the changing and growing needs of the University, leading to the creation of an Academic Support team, managed by an Assistant Director (Academic Support). Copyright is now part of this team alongside the institutional repository and subject liaison librarians, which provides comprehensive support to the University's learning, teaching and research aims and objectives.

The Copyright Officer works closely with the Systems Support team responsible for Electronic Resources, e-strategy and library systems, and with the Resource Development team within the Library, who manage interlibrary loans, reading list processing and acquisitions. Within the institution, there are close links with Registry, Computing and Media Services and the e-Learning team, as well as directly with academic staff within Schools. The role therefore involves working with a wide variety of colleagues at many levels.

Role and responsibilities

The role deals primarily with the following areas:

- copyright licence administration
- creating and implementing copyright policy and procedures
- copyright compliance monitoring
- copyright clearance
- copyright consultancy (guidance on copyright and IPR issues, with a focus on digital copyright)
- designing and delivering staff development and user education on copyright and IPR in a teaching, learning and research environment.

The Copyright Officer is responsible for ensuring that the University meets the requirements of copyright law by administering licences and providing advice and training. The role directly supports the University's e-learning strategy, playing a significant role in making digital resources of all kinds available to staff and students, developing services and helping to ensure that initiatives in this area are seamlessly integrated from a user's perspective. The Digital Readings Service, which delivers digital readings licensed by CLA to the VLE, is one such initiative.

Core parts of the role of the Copyright Officer are ensuring that staff and students are aware of the terms of the licences, developing support materials and disseminating information in the form of web pages, staff development sessions, handbooks and newsletters. Copyright clearance is perhaps the smallest part of the role, possibly because Brunel encourage and provide support to staff to obtain their own, and before the post was created, many staff and departments were accustomed to doing this themselves.

Problems, issues, challenges

The key areas of difficulty relate to the CLA Licence almost exclusively. The licence terms and conditions are complex, requiring interpretation or condensing into manageable bite-sized formats for staff. This requires a heavy programme of training, which has been embedded in the training programme for staff learning to use the VLE. The VLE was upgraded to a new version in 2007, which required training for most staff, and 50 sessions were delivered to staff during that year. The programme has lessened, but it is expected that the training workload will increase in 2010, when an upgrade is planned to improve functionality.

Brunel has found that academic staff, who are the primary users of the licence in their teaching, and to a lesser extent in their research, simply do not have the time to absorb the complexities of the licence and work out how to apply them to their needs. Many staff are balancing heavy teaching, research and administrative workloads and the reality for most is that planning course content and relevant readings is often done under pressure. It is not uncommon for reading lists to be put together on an ad-hoc basis, even a week before they are needed. In fact, from an academic's viewpoint, it is arguably the best method to guarantee the currency and relevance of readings, although from a library perspective this is the worst possible way, as the acquisitions process takes time, particularly when many lists come in at once.

It is somewhat easier to say that everything that is shared in any electronic environment requires copyright clearance as without a CLA Licence this is the case. Having the CLA Licence has complicated the situation tremendously, as sometimes only part of the copyright message is retained – which leads to omissions in reporting from academics who use the licence, leading to double the amount of time spent carrying out retrospective licence compliance checks. Much content used is not even part of the CLA Licence repertoire, although often it is covered by some other licence, for example e-journals. However the time must be invested to verify this.

Conclusion

Compliance with multiple terms and conditions in complex licences is resource-intensive and the workload it generates increases exponentially each year with increasing use of e-learning environments and other emerging technologies where the rules are different.

Overall, even with a dedicated post, it is a very challenging task to ensure that the institution complies with copyright legislation and terms of 'blanket' and contractual licensing which are not yet flexible enough to allow academics to make use of the best resources available, without getting bogged down in working out what is legal or not. At Brunel the view is that copyright can hamper the ability to teach, which has an impact on the creative output of students and researchers and ultimately on the economy.

Ireland

Irish copyright laws are broadly similar to the UK although the Copyright and Related Rights Act dates from 2000. Educational institutions are mandated to take out a licence to cover multiple copying of copyright works from the Irish Copyright Licensing Agency (ICLA) (www.icla.ie). Licences are available for the primary and secondary sectors and also for higher education. The licence also covers digital copying of Irish works for secondary schools and for the higher education sector. However, several Irish institutions are still unsure about whether the licence enables them to put materials onto a VLE, because of some of the terms of the CLA

Licence. The licence specifies that institutions can make 'digital copies' (defined as scanning unaltered from the original) of copyright works:

◆ already owned by the institution
◆ not exceeding the limits of the paper licence (that is, 5% or chapter of a book, one article from a journal, a short story or poem not exceeding 10 pages from an anthology)
◆ not including printed music, newspapers, maps, charts, books of tables, artistic work other than that essential to illustrate a text, in-house journals, or 'privately prepared teaching materials'.

The licence also specifies that:

◆ no changing/editing of the material is permitted
◆ digital copies should not be posted on the web or sent by e-mail or linked to such that it can be accessed by unauthorized parties
◆ no copying to storage devices of the digital materials is permitted
◆ gathering of the copies is only permissible for backup purposes and not for construction of a repository/database of resources.

Scanning under the licence is currently causing concerns in some Irish institutions who are concerned that they might not be able to restrict users from copying the files to a storage device – such as a Universal Serial Bus (USB) stick, or their own computer. On the positive side, one of the key differences of Irish copyright law to copyright law in the UK is the recent amendment that now means that licences and contracts for digital publications (such as electronic journals or databases) cannot limit the exceptions to copyright (such as fair dealing) provided by statute.

Australia

In Australia the Copyright Act 1968 remains in force although significant changes were made to the law in 2000, which impacted on the copying that could be undertaken for educational purposes. Specifically the Copyright Amendment (Digital Agenda) Act 2000 meant that from 2001 it has been possible to scan copyright works for educational purposes under a licence from the reprographic rights organization, Copyright Agency Limited

(CAL). The CAL website (www.copyright.com.au) provides guidance for those in education and the education licences are blanket licences similar to that issued in the UK in 2005. Two licences are offered, the first known as the Hardcopy Licence covers photocopying, scanning from print or re-keying print resources and storing them in digital format. Meanwhile the Electronic Reproduction and Communication licence covers digital-to-digital copying and digital-to-paper copying. The similarity of these licences with those which are offered in the UK is largely a reflection of the similarities of the legislative environment.

The CAL licences are more permissive than the CLA Licence in the UK, permitting 10% of a literary or musical work to be copied or one article from a journal issue. Artistic works can be copied in their entirety and copying from the web and CD-ROM are also covered by the Electronic licence. Copies can only be distributed to registered students on a course and the material must also contain a copyright statement. Where the CAL licences also differs from the UK is in the provision for data reporting. Whereas UK universities have agreed to full data reporting on all items they scan under licence since 2005, data reporting is not a requirement of the Australian licence and compliance is monitored largely through periodic surveys. Further information about the CAL Licences is available from their website and they also include Frequently Asked Questions (CAL, 2009).

New Zealand

Although the New Zealand Copyright Act 1994 allows schools, public tertiary institutions and non-profit private training establishments to copy material from published works for educational purposes, the amounts permitted are limited. Therefore New Zealand has a similar licensing scheme to permit copying beyond these limits issued by Copyright Licensing Limited (CLL) (www.copyright.co.nz). CLL is the reprographic rights organization in New Zealand and offers licences for education and other sectors. Scanning under the Copyright Licensing Limited licence in a HEI features in a case study from the University of Auckland presented in Chapter 4. The licence is similar to the Australian licence in terms of the limits being 10% of a work. Sample data is collected from selected licensees over an eight-week period when full records need to be kept. Outside this time full data reporting is not a requirement of the licence. Further sources of advice about New Zealand copyright law are included in the Conclusion, but both the Copyright Council of New Zealand and the Library and Information Association of New Zealand Aotearoa (LIANZA) provide useful information.

Canada

Canadian copyright laws are based on UK law, thus principles such as fair dealing exist and there are similar exceptions to copyright for educational purposes. Since 2007 the Canadian government has been attempting to review its copyright laws, which has led to considerable public concern about copyright issues. Known as C-61 the reforms were criticized by many including Michael Geist a University of Ottawa law professor, who led a movement that gained enormous popularity through a Facebook group. For example, amendments to Canadian law to outlaw the circumvention of digital rights managements systems have been met with much opposition. Campaigners argue that circumvention for non-infringing purposes, such as fair dealing or uses permitted by educational and library exceptions in the Copyright Act, must be allowed.

The Gatineau Copyright Roundtable was held in July 2009 and attended by copyright experts and representatives from bodies such as the Association of Universities and Colleges of Canada (AUCC). The AUCC recognized, in particular, that copyright reforms were needed to support e-learning, stating that educational uses of materials freely posted on the internet should be permitted, and that:

> Copyright law must also be amended to facilitate technology enhanced learning so that students participating in a program of learning through the Internet will not be disadvantaged in comparison with their counterparts physically present in the classroom, and educational institutions will be able to take advantage of new information and communications technologies for program delivery.
>
> (AUCC, 2009)

There are several resources on Canadian copyright law listed in the

Conclusion. The Canadian Library Association maintain a Copyright Information Centre on their website and are another good source of up-to-date information.

The USA

In the United States the copyright legislation dates from 1974, but several other acts have been issued that those working in education need to be aware of. If we first consider the Copyright Act 1974, copying for education under this act is certainly less restrictive than other countries in the world. The concept of 'fair use' is enshrined in the law, and differs substantially from the similar sounding 'fair dealing'. Specifically 'fair use' covers copying for educational purposes. In the late 1990s many US librarians were involved in CONFU (Conference on Fair Use) to set out guidelines of what could be copied under this provision. This coincided with many university libraries establishing electronic reserves services. Electronic reserves are either scanned or digital copies of copyright works made available to students via the library. Taken from the US term for short loan collections, traditional paper 'reserves' were either books or copies of articles kept in the library to facilitate teaching. Electronic reserves services were originally separate to the development of e-learning systems, but increasingly these services are now integrated. Some US universities rely on the fair use provision to deliver copyright material to students, and only seek copyright permission for material that is repeatedly used in a course of study. Others are more risk averse and will routinely seek permission to digitize material for electronic reserves either directly with publishers or through the US reprographic rights organization, the Copyright Clearance Center (CCC). The CCC also now offer a blanket licence to institutions who wish to cover the copying they undertake.

Other relevant US legislation

The Digital Millennium Copyright Act (DCMA) came into force in 1998 and specifically prohibits the circumvention of any 'technological protection measure' that a copyright owner might put in place. This means that digital material that a teacher might legitimately wish to use in teaching may be prohibited if a publisher had placed some form of digital rights management provision in place. Meanwhile legislation dating from 2002 has also impacted on the delivery of copyright works in the US, specifically with relation to distance learners. The TEACH (Technology, Education and Copyright Harmonization) Act allows copyright works to be delivered to distance learners without permission from the rights holder and without the payment of fees. It covers the digitization of analogue works to produce digital materials if a digital version is not available for purchase.

Some of the specific requirements of this act include:

◆ only not-for-profit educational institutions are covered
◆ they must have an institutional copyright policy
◆ they must provide copyright information to faculty, other staff and students
◆ the material must have a notice to inform students of the copyright policy
◆ the materials can only be distributed to enrolled students.

The TEACH act formalized what had been, until this point, a grey area in US legislation. It allowed US institutions to make digital copies of published content available to students via a secure network. However, activity in this area has not been without controversy and only recently have large publishing houses embarked on legal action against universities that they believed to be in breach of copyright. The University of California and Georgia State University are two universities that were recently pursued in court by publishers who believed their copyright had been infringed. Case Study 3 examines practice at one US university which takes a less risk adverse approach to copyright issues.

Copyright and scholarly communication

While technology moves at a fast pace and offers teachers greater possibilities in terms of delivering different types of resources to students across a network, copyright law is often perceived as being slow to change and out of step with what is now technically possible. Arguably copying material for educational purposes has also been an area of unspoken tension between publishers and academics. Many academic authors are themselves rights holders and as content creators they wish to see their work protected and derive a modest income from their publications. However, the nature of education means that reproducing, copying, modifying and amending the work of others has always been a fundamental part of scholarship. Very little research is undertaken without building on the findings of previous studies and conventions such as citation and referencing were developed to recognize and acknowledge the works of others. So it is inevitable that teachers will use others ideas in the classroom, particularly in the arts, humanities and social sciences, where debate, opinion and argument are a fundamental part of the learning process. However, technology has led many in the industries of publishing, film and music to try to tighten copyright laws further still. In the face of ever tighter copyright restrictions some academics and IPR experts have launched initiatives to attempt to redress the imbalance that they believe now exists. A few of these initiatives are worthy of mention and discussed briefly next.

Creative Commons

The Creative Commons (CC) movement was founded in 2001 by Lawrence Lessig and a group of cyberlaw and intellectual property rights experts. Lessig is a Professor of Law at Stanford Law School and founder of the school's Center for Internet and Society. The movement, sometimes called an alternative to copyright, is founded on the belief that modern copyright laws have become overly restrictive and are stifling creativity. According to their website (Creative Commons, 2009): 'A single goal unites Creative Commons' current and future projects: to build a layer of reasonable, flexible copyright in the face of increasingly restrictive default rules.'

Creative Commons is also referred to as 'some rights reserved' meaning that content creators can attach licences to their work to indicate that they are happy for it to be used in certain circumstances. Different licences exist, including Attribution, Non-commercial/commercial and Share Alike. As a content creator, a teacher can attach a Creative Commons License to their work to indicate that they are happy to share it under certain conditions. Teachers can also use the Creative Commons search to identify material that they can use in their teaching. Specific Creative Commons Licenses are available for different jurisdiction around the world. For example the

UK: England and Wales licences are available from their website: http://creativecommons.org/international/uk. You can also find out more about the progress of the licences in different countries around the world from: http://creativecommons.org/international.

Open access and open education resources

A parallel development related to Creative Commons, which has done much work recently to raise awareness about copyright issues has been the open access and open educational resources (OER) movement, led by institutions such as the Massachusetts Institute of Technology (MIT). Suber (2007) provides a useful definition stating: 'Open-access (OA) literature is digital, online, free of charge, and free of most copyright and licensing restrictions.' Suber provides a valuable overview of the open access movement, which is largely beyond the scope of this book. However, the establishment of open access repositories to capture the intellectual output of researchers by HEIs has done much to highlight the importance of copyright issues. Many higher education funding councils are now mandating authors to deposit publicly funded research outputs into an open access repository. Additionally, academics are starting to question whether they should assign copyright of their own publications to a publisher. One of the biggest concerns of the open access movement has been the restrictive licensing models of large publishers that effectively lock the general public out of accessing the outputs of publicly funded research. Many in the open access movement maintain it is not anti- copyright. In fact websites such as the SHERPA RoMEO website (University of Nottingham, 2008), developed by JISC and hosted by the University of Nottingham, have done much to raise awareness of publishers' copyright policies and help ensure that content deposited in open access repositories is there with permission from the publisher. A key advantage of open access publications for the e-learning community is that research output can be used (often by simply linking to it) without the need to pay additional permission fees to publishers.

Related to this are open educational resources, which are described by the United Nations Educational, Scientific and Cultural Organization (UNESCO) (2002) as:

technology-enabled, open provision of educational resources for consultation, use and adaptation by a community of users for non-commercial purposes. . . . They are typically made freely available over the Web or the Internet. Their principal use is by teachers and educational institutions to support course development, but they can also be used directly by students' and described by the Organisation for Economic Co-operation and Development (OECD) as, 'digitised materials offered freely and openly for educators, students and self-learners to use and reuse for teaching, learning and research'.

(OECD, 2007)

It is important to be clear on the distinction between the terms 'free' and 'open' and how they are used together in this context. 'Free' materials may be offered for no cost but under strict copyright protection without permission to repurpose, adapt and reuse. 'Open' educational materials are deliberately licensed by the creator for reuse by others, sometimes without the need to reference the original author, and without restriction on how and in what context the materials can be used. However, free materials, even online, are not necessarily open. Open Educational Resources are discussed in more detail in Case Study 4 (see pages 75–80).

Open-source software

It is worth briefly mentioning open-source software and how this relates to e-learning and copyright issues. Open-source software is defined by the Open-source Initiative (OSI, 2009) and needs to meet ten criteria, including: free distribution, access to the source code and a free licence to distribute the software. Open-source software is an alternative to commercial, proprietary software and has much in common with Creative Commons and the open access movement, in terms of challenging more traditional licensing models. Increasing numbers of institutions are considering open-source solutions for e-learning; for example, the open-source VLE Moodle is widely used in higher and further education. A growing number of open-source learning tools are also available such as VLEs, e-portfolio software, social networking tools, and content management systems. While this development is separate to the other movements discussed earlier, it is related to a desire by some institutions to have a greater control over the software that they use and the licensing fees that they are charged.

Conclusion

This chapter first explored what e-learning is and how teachers might wish to use content in the digital environment. It also considered how e-learning differs from classroom teaching and why copyright issues are more pertinent. It has also examined how the UK and several other countries approach copyright and how this impacts on online education. The chapter has shown how developments in technology are necessitating reforms to the existing copyright legislation throughout the world. In many countries a satisfactory balance has yet to be achieved between protecting the economic well-being of rights holders and the needs of educators to be able to share, copy and disseminate information freely.

References

ACRL Statement on Fair Use and Electronic Reserves, www.ala.org/ala/mgrps/divs/acrl/publications/whitepapers/statementfair.cfm [accessed 10 January 2010].

AUCC (2009) *Advocacy and Research: Copyright*, www.aucc.ca/policy/issues/copyright_e.html [accessed 10 January 2010].

Becta (2009a) *Becta's role*, http://about.becta.org.uk/ [accessed 10 January 2010].

Becta (2009b) *What is a Learning Platform?* http://schools.becta.org.uk/index.php?section=lv&catcode=ss_lv_lp_03&rid=12887 [accessed 10 January 2010].CAL (2009)

Copyright Agency Limited: FAQs for copyright users, www.copyright.com.au/Copyright_Users/FAQs/FAQs_for_copyright_users.aspx [accessed 10 January 2010].

Cornish, Graham (2009) *Copyright: interpreting the law for libraries, archives and information services*, 5th edn, Facet Publishing.

Creative Commons (2009), http://wiki.creativecommons.org/History

DCMS (2009) Digital Economy Bill: a punishing future, *Guardian*, 23 Nov, www.guardian.co.uk/commentisfree/2009/nov/23/editorial-digital-economy-bill [accessed 10 January 2010].

DfEs (2005) *Harnessing Technology: transforming learning and children's services*, www.dcsf.gov.uk/elearningstrategy [accessed 10 January 2010].

HM Treasury (2006) *Report on Gowers Review,*
http://webarchive.nationalarchives.gov.uk/+/www.hm-
treasury.gov.uk/d/pbr06_gowers_report_755.pdf [accessed 10
January 2010].

Intellectual Property Office (2008) *Copyright Abroad,*
www.ipo.gov.uk/types/copy/c-abroad.htm [accessed 10 January
2010].

McCracken, R. (2007) *Gowers Review: the OU response*. Presentation given
at the BUVFC Learning On Screen Conference. British Library, 2
April 2007.

Norman, S. (2004) *Practical Copyright for Information Professionals: the
CILIP handbook,* Facet Publishing.

OECD (2007) *Giving Knowledge for Free: the emergence of open educational
resources,*
www.oecd.org/document/41/0,3343,en_2649_35845581_38659497_1_1
_1_1,00.html [accessed 5 January 2010].

Open-source Initiative (OSI) (2009) *Open-source Definition,*
www.opensource.org/docs/osd.

OPSI (2002) *Copyright (Visually Impaired Persons) Act 2002,*
www.opsi.gov.uk/ACTS/acts2002/ukpga_20020033_en_1 [accessed 10
January 2010].

OPSI (2003) Statutory Instrument 2003 No. 2498. *The Copyright and
Related Rights,*
www.opsi.gov.uk/si/si2003/20032498.htm [accessed 10 January 2010].

OPSI (2009) Copyright, Designs and Patents Act 1988,
www.opsi.gov.uk/acts/acts1988/UKpga_19880048_en_1.htm
[accessed 10 January 2010].

Pedley, P. (2007) *Digital Copyright,* 2nd edn, Facet Publishing.

Reference for TEACH Act from ALA,
www.ala.org/Template.cfm?Section=distanced&Template=/Content
Management/ContentDisplay.cfm&ContentID=25939 [accessed 10
January 2010].

RIN (2007) *Researchers' Use of Academic Libraries and their Services.*

Rowlands, I., Nicholas, D., Williams, P., Huntington, P., Fieldhouse, M.,
Gunter, B., Withey, R., Jamali, H.R., Dobrowolski, T. and Tenopir, C.
(2008) The Google Generation: the information behaviour of the
researcher of the future, *Aslib Proceedings,* 60 (4), 290-310.

Rusbridge, C. (1998) Towards the Hybrid Library, *D-Lib Magazine* (July/Aug),
www.dlib.org/dlib/july98/rusbridge/07rusbridge.html [accessed 8 Jan 2010].

SCONUL (2009, August 4th) *SCONUL calls for fair deal for university libraries over copyright law*,
www.sconul.ac.uk/news/lammy [accessed 10 January 2010].

Secker, J. (2004) *Electronic Resources in the Virtual Learning Environment: a guide for librarians*, Chandos.

Suber, P. (2007) *Open Access Overview*,
www.earlham.edu/~peters/fos/overview.htm [accessed 10 January 2010].

UNESCO (2002) *UNESCO Promotes New Initiative for Free Educational Resources on the Internet*,
www.unesco.org/education/news_en/080702_free_edu_ress.shtml [accessed 5 January 2010].

University of Nottingham (2008), *SHERPA RoMEO: publisher copyright policies and self-archiving*,
www.sherpa.ac.uk/romeo [accessed 10 January 2010].

2 Digitizing published content for delivery in the VLE

Introduction

This chapter is concerned with the copyright issues associated with digitizing or scanning published materials (such as books and academic journals) for delivery via an e-learning system. Digitizing traditional paper resources for online delivery allows distance learners to easily access the content from the convenience of their desktop. However, there has been a growing demand from campus-based students to have access to core readings in electronic format. Library statistics from groups such as SCONUL demonstrate that campus-based students visit academic libraries less frequently and tend to concentrate on readings that are provided to them in digital format. This is partly a reflection of the changing nature of students, with far greater numbers now studying part-time and many working while they study. It is also related to the different expectations of young people about how they access information, as discussed in Chapter 1. Libraries are responding to increased demands for digital readings and now find it increasingly easy to produce digital readings in-house, with scanners now being inexpensive to purchase. Some libraries are also motivated by a desire to reduce the physical size of the library collection.

In the UK, the provision of core readings in scanned format has escalated recently, largely facilitated by the inclusion of scanning rights in the Copyright Licensing Agency blanket licences. All three of the schools, further and higher education licences allow institutions to digitize copyright material in addition to photocopying. Scanning rights were first introduced into the business and further education sectors in 2004. However, in higher education the CLA are closely monitoring this activity by mandating institutions to report details of all the scanning on an annual basis. Despite this requirement, since the licence was issued in 2005, HEIs in the UK are scanning a large number of readings largely for delivery via e-learning systems. This chapter presents further details of this activity, collected through a recent survey. It explores how scanned readings are being used to support e-learning and how copyright issues are increasing the administrative processes in higher education libraries.

As we saw in Chapter 1, in various other countries around the world, the reprographic rights organizations are also issuing licences to cover scanning copyright materials. For example, New Zealand, Australia and Ireland all have similar licences. However, only in the UK have rights holders insisted on full data reporting to monitor every reading that is scanned for use in higher education. This chapter will briefly consider how universities in the United States digitize published content either under copyright exceptions or consequent of licences. However this chapter does not seek to be comprehensive in examining other countries in the world. The focus instead is on how legislation and licences regulate activity in this area and shape e-learning in different countries.

Finally this chapter also briefly discusses the digitization of unpublished materials, including historical or archival materials where direct permissions usually need to be obtained from rights holders. It also considers how to deal with items where rights holders cannot be traced. These are frequently referred to as 'orphan works'. For reasons of clarity, the use of existing digital resources (sometimes called 'born digital content') such as e-journal articles or e-books is discussed in Chapter 3, along with the use of digital content obtained from websites, repositories or materials acquired from colleagues.

Using published materials in e-learning

Copyright issues invariably arise when teachers want to scan or digitize content for use in an online course. Many resources that are uploaded into an e-learning system are owned by the teacher or their respective institution; however it is common for teachers to want to use materials that are owned by an organization such as a publisher. This type of content is often called 'third-party material' due to it being owned by neither the author nor the institution but a 'third-party'. While some teachers, particularly in higher education, might be keen to create all their content from scratch, this is rarely practical or desirable all the time. Moreover, in a college or university, while teaching materials (such as PowerPoint presentations, class handouts and lecture notes) are usually created by the lecturer, s/he often wants to include content from external authoritative sources such as books and journals. However, due to the nature of scholarly publishing, the copyright of journal articles is usually assigned through a contract to the publisher. Even when publishing a monograph, academic authors frequently share copyright with their publisher and will be required as a courtesy to notify their publisher if they want to make the final published content available to their students. While the open access movement, discussed in Chapter 1, has done much to highlight this issue, many academic authors are still signing contracts with publishers that mean that their content cannot be used in e-learning in its final published version without copyright permission. In the past, negotiating contracts or licences to published content was common place when building an e-learning course that relied on third-party content. In recent years blanket licences issued by reprographic organizations have been extremely helpful meaning that there is less of a need to secure permissions through negotiating with individual publishers. This process can be time-consuming and very few educational establishments have designated staff to carry out this work. Therefore blanket licences have meant more and more educational establishments can include published content in their virtual learning environment.

By far the most common type of content that educators wish to include in e-learning is published content from books, journals, magazines or newspapers. It is standard practice to expect someone undertaking a course of study to do 'further reading' and to provide them with a reading list. In a digital environment it is the logical next step to not just suggest what the student should read, but actually provide them with a digital copy of the text. If the students are distance learners, the teacher may feel some of the resources will be difficult to obtain by students who may not have easy access to an academic library. Meanwhile in some subject disciplines, such as history or English literature, the teacher may wish students to consult archival sources and so digitization can provide access to otherwise unobtainable material. For some academics (and students) e-learning has become synonymous with digital access to content and while many learning technologists try to encourage academics to make their courses more interactive, VLEs are often largely an online document store.

Desktop scanners are now extremely cheap to purchase and the production of a digital copy of a printed document is often as straightforward as photocopying an item. Increasingly photocopier-scanners have the facility to produce a digital file with great ease. However, scanning or digitizing a work and distributing a digital file such as a PDF via a network is a restricted act under most copyright laws and the exclusive right of the copyright owner. Only in the United States, where 'fair use' covers educational copying might an institution undertake this practice, and then specific guidelines govern what is permitted. Yet, many educators wrongly believe that they are exempt from such laws if they place the content on a secure network, restricted to students on a course of study or protected with a password. This is rarely the case, as we shall see in this chapter.

Scanning published content in the UK

This chapter examines scanning in higher education in the UK to support e-learning in some detail. It includes results from a recent survey that highlight how the CLA Licence has affected the support for e-learning that institutions can now provide, for the licence enables digitized content to be used in virtual learning environments. While third-party content is not vital to the success of e-learning, in an increasingly global education market, differences in copyright law do make it easier for some countries to provide their students with published content. It is also inevitable that confusion and misunderstandings can occur particularly when teachers move to other countries to teach and find that the law is not consistent. This chapter should provide a useful overview for teachers in higher education in the UK to help them stay within the law and licensing guidelines. It also highlights how the legal framework is influencing the nature of e-learning and impacting on higher education.

The UK has relatively liberal copyright laws in terms of the exceptions that apply under the Copyright, Designs and Patents Act 1988. Unfortunately one area where UK law is not strong is in terms of the copying that is permitted for educational purposes. While a provision for educational copying is in the UK legislation (Sections 32–36), in reality most multiple copying for teaching purposes is actually done under licences, such as those issued by the Copyright Licensing Agency. This is because the law prevents copying by a 'reprographic process' and limits the number of copies that can be made to one. While single copies can be made for non-commercial private study and research, this right is not extended to teachers making multiple copies, except in very small numbers. Regardless of these provisions, UK law also states that where a licensing scheme exists, this takes precedence.

UK law sets out a provision known as 'fair dealing' (frequently confused by US academics and teachers as being the same as 'fair use' – see page 24). Copying of a work can be undertaken under fair dealing for private study and research, but also for criticism and review. However, in reality very few educational establishments would rely on fair dealing as a defence for putting material on a network, because only single copies are permitted. Therefore, much educational copying is undertaken under a CLA Licence and all universities and most schools and colleges take out such a licence to cover their staff.

Background and context

The Copyright Licensing Agency is the UK's reprographic rights organization, representing publishers, authors and other rights owners of published books and journals. Since 1984 they have issued licences to facilitate copying beyond the provisions in UK law and their first blanket licences for the educational sector were issued in 1986 (CLA, 2009a).

Digitization of copyright materials were first explored in some detail by the Joint Information Systems Committee. They funded several projects under their eLib programme in the mid to late 1990s to explore copyright issues associated with digitizing core readings for students. Projects such as ACORN (Access to COurse Readings via Networks) and SCOPE (Scottish Collaborative On-demand Publishing Enterprise) had looked at the feasibility of setting up electronic short loan services, but every item had to be cleared directly with a publisher. In 1998 JISC and Blackwells set up a project into service known as Higher Education Resources ONdemand to offer copyright clearance and digitization services for the sector. The work of HERON was greatly facilitated in 1999, when the CLA became the world's first reprographic rights organization to issue a digitization licence, albeit as a transactional licence. Items covered by the CLA Licence could be cleared via a service known as CLA Rapid Clearance Service (CLARCS).

Between 1999 and 2005 approximately 80 universities joined HERON which acted as a clearing house for permissions, and digitized materials on behalf of the institutions. Under the first CLA digitization licence prices for copyright clearance were based on the numbers of pages of an article or chapter and the number of students on a course of study. Despite an agreement between the Publishers Association and JISC that recommended the rate was set at five pence per page per student, in reality the costs were far higher. Some universities were unable or unwilling to pay for clearances of a transactional nature and never joined the HERON service. A few decided to carry out the copyright clearance and digitization in-house.

In addition to obtaining permission for digital copies, universities had been using the CLARCS service to clear paper course packs since 1998. The need to clear permissions was causing problems for many universities and in 2000, Universities UK (who represent the sector as a whole) referred the terms of the higher education licence to the Copyright Tribunal. The subsequent ruling in 2002 led to the abolishment of the CLARCS service for paper course packs and a less than favourable view of transactional licences.

Negotiations towards a blanket digitization licence were time-consuming, and after lengthy debates between UUK and CLA, the trial scanning licence was initially launched in 2005. The licence was an optional addition to the CLA higher education photocopying licence and, priced at 50 pence per student, was considered by many institutions to be expensive. At this time CLA insisted on the full reporting of items that were digitized for those who took up the trial. In 2008 following again lengthy negotiations, CLA and UUK agreed a Blanket Scanning and Photocopying licence that will run until August 2011. The licence took two forms, the Comprehensive Licence, which covered photocopying, scanning and the use of digital originals, and the Basic licence which includes photocopying and scanning. Further details of both these licences are available from the CLA website (CLA, 2009b). One proviso from the CLA was that full reporting of scanned items and digital originals was maintained. Consequently many institutions have been dissatisfied with the administrative burden they feel that this places on their staff. This burden has largely been shouldered by academic libraries, rather than e-learning teams, as libraries hold the published works, usually have greater staff numbers and are responsible for providing access to this type of content.

The HERON service still exists today, now owned by Publishing Technology Ltd. While fewer universities are still members, it still provides copyright clearance and digitization services under the CLA Licence, but also for material outside the licence that requires clearance with a publisher. Some universities in the UK use the rights management system PackTracker, developed by HERON, which greatly speeds up the reporting of scanned items to the CLA. This system allows an institution to record details of scanned items (transactions) that relate to a specific course of study. The processing of requests can be managed to record when items need scanning and when an item might need renewing. Copyright coversheets can also be generated as can the spreadsheet which needs to be sent to the CLA detailing all scanning under their licence. The use of PackTracker at UCL is described in more detail in the case study that follows.

Case Study 2: UCL library services' course reading service, UK

June Hedges

UCL Context

The University College London is London's leading multidisciplinary university, with 8000 staff and some 22,000 students. Teaching and research extends across all academic disciplines. Despite the strong focus on research, UCL is committed to supporting excellent learning and teaching to the taught course students who represent more than three-quarters of the student body.

Taught course support at UCL

UCL is one of only a handful of UK universities that has a dedicated team within Library Services to support the needs of taught course students. The Teaching & Learning Support Section (TLSS) was established in 1996 as a result of a study into how the Library could best support taught courses in light of an increase in student numbers. The services provided by the TLSS aim to enable maximum access to core resources required by students on taught courses, and focus on:

- managing and creating online versions of reading lists
- creating digital and print copies of extracts recommended on course reading lists
- creating print 'study packs' – bound printed packs containing copies of core readings for a particular course.

The TLSS team, comprising of 3 full-time professional librarians, 1.6 FTE clerical assistants and 40 hours of assistant time (typically student workers), is relatively small considering the size of the community it supports. However, the current team has almost doubled in size since 1995.

Evolving a course reading service

The TLSS has always relied heavily on the blanket licensing scheme provided by the CLA to increase access to core readings. Initially this was through the Higher Education Photocopying Licence, but with the increased emphasis of online resources in the last six years the demand for digital copies has grown. The launch of the CLA Trial Digitization Licence in 2005 gave the TLSS the opportunity to start addressing this demand – without a blanket licence in place and with no dedicated budget, transactional permissions to scan readings had not proved feasible. From 2005 onwards TLSS has gradually moved away from providing paper copy to offering digital files wherever possible. This has included retrospective digitization of the existing paper course readings held in the Library short loan collections.

The introduction of digital course readings also allowed TLSS to refocus its services and move toward a single 'Course Reading Service', which incorporated the existing online reading list service with the provision of core digital readings. The online reading list system, which underpins the service, enables direct linking to existing e-resources, such as journal articles and web-based reports, thus taking advantage of all manner of electronic resources that are provided by the Library or are freely available on the web.

Making course readings available

All work to support the delivery of scanned course readings at UCL is handled in-house, including copyright checking and digitization. The processes used evolved initially out of existing paper services, but with a steady increase in demand for readings and a growing team handling requests, a robust set of procedures and specialist software were required.

The PackTracker software, provided by HERON, was implemented at UCL in 2004 to streamline the management of paper services, but also with an eye to providing digital readings in the future. PackTracker ensures that all materials related to a single course are recorded in one place and allows the team to manage the workflow process effectively. The software works by creating a 'Pack' for each module and readings associated with the module are added to each pack as 'transactions'. Each transaction is given a unique identifier which also becomes the extract's filename when the reading has been scanned. The main benefit of PackTracker is that progress with each reading can be recorded and tracked easily. PackTracker also adds the coversheet required by the CLA Licence to each reading, as well as recording and formatting all scanning data required for the annual CLA data report.

Typically, the production of a scanned reading is instigated by a lecturer, who provides bibliographic details of the reading together with a photocopy of the item. In some instances a complete list of readings is submitted which is then checked to see which readings can be scanned before the lecturer makes copies. The advertised turnaround time is six weeks to allow the team to cope with demand prior to the start of a term.

On receipt of a digital reading request, the process proceeds as follows:

1   Photocopy and accompanying Submission Form are received in TLSS and logged with date of receipt.
    —   *The form includes brief details of the terms and limits of the CLA Licence, required fields relating to the bibliographic details of the extract being submitted and the module for which it is to be made available (module code and student numbers).*
2   The extract is checked for compliance with the CLA Licence, the Submission form is annotated according to whether the extract can be scanned, or has to be made available in a paper collection, or if there are queries to send back to the lecturer. Extracts that fall completely outside of the Licence are returned to lecturers with a suggestion that they may wish to substitute it for an alternative.

3   The item is added to PackTracker. This may involve creating a new 'pack' with the details of the module for which the reading is to be made available. The items' bibliographic details are recorded along with internal processing information, for example, that the item is to be scanned.
4   The photocopy is scanned in-house straight to PDF. Currently the files are image PDFs; the OCR process proved too time-consuming for the volume of work handled by TLSS. However, the team is monitoring OCR software and would consider converting files to text PDF if the accuracy rates improved. A coversheet is generated by PackTracker, added to the file and is then uploaded to a secure server. An assistant will then usually add a link to the reading to an online reading list, or if a lecturer is not using this service, will send them a link to add to the VLE module (UCL uses Moodle).
5   The photocopy is returned to the lecturer.

Without a central budget, material that falls outside of the CLA Licence is not usually made available. However, with a strategic aim to deliver course materials digitally wherever possible UCL has begun to trial the use of a budget previously used to pay for multiple copies of core texts to fund transactional permissions. This trial began in October 2009 and take up so far has been small. This is in part due to the fact that lecturers using the service are familiar with the limits of the CLA Licence and tend not to submit materials they know will not qualify for scanning, but also due to many permission fees still being higher than the cost of purchasing multiple copies of hard copy rather than committing to recurrent permission fees.

Statistics

Figure 2.1 below illustrates the growth in demand for course readings overall and also the sharp decline in the number of paper readings that are processed.

Support for e-learning

The growth in the popularity of e-learning across UCL has created a greater demand for digital resources which goes far beyond digital copies of core readings to support teaching. With this demand the need for guidance on all manner of copyright issues ranging from the reuse of third-party materials to

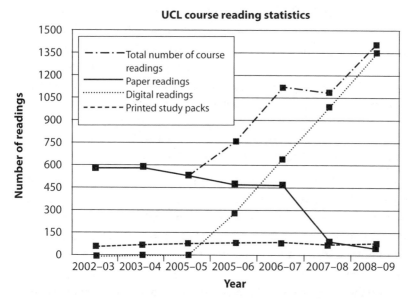

Figure 2.1 *Graph to illustrate growth in demand for course readings at UCL*

the protection of individuals own work and content has risen sharply. As teaching staff are encouraged to use the VLE they are also expected to ensure that materials are used legally. The TLSS with its expertise in the area of using materials for teaching is a natural focus for copyright queries. They receive queries about the reuse of materials from all manner of sources directly from lecturers and they also provide training on copyright issues for staff using the VLE. The training covers areas such as basic information on copyright, how to find materials that can be reused without permission (for example, materials made available under Creative Common Licensing), how to check whether permission is needed for reuse and how permission can be obtained when it is required. To reinforce this, TLSS provide web-based guidelines, which include templates for requesting permission for materials.

Alongside processing requests for digital readings, TLSS provide support for lecturers who wish to use non-textual resources. Often they would like to reuse materials already on web pages, in which case the team suggest that they pursue the request themselves using a template. However, where a permission request may be more complex, or involve a fee, TLSS will handle clearances on their behalf. For example, in the case of a selection of ethnographic films to be streamed and linked into a VLE module to support a Masters anthropology course, at the lecturer's request, TLSS contacted various film-making bodies to request permission to reuse that material and relayed information back to the lecturer regarding permission fees and any other conditions stipulated by the owner. In other cases TLSS advise on copyright issues related to the possible digitization of particular types of resources; for instance, converting the History of Art Department's analogue slide collection to digital format.

Conclusion : issues facing the TLSS

The popularity of the service increases despite little marketing and consequently the number of new requests for scanned readings has risen each year. Alongside this sits the burden of renewing existing readings, which even with PackTracker to manage the process, is labour-intensive. UCL have not yet limited the number of readings that can be scanned, but this may become necessary in the future.

Handling the clearance of materials either not in print format or not covered by a blanket licensing scheme is set to grow, particularly as the onus is put on lecturers to ensure that they are using materials legally. This will entail developing new expertise and new procedures to track requests, but also a considerable amount of awareness-raising on the part of lecturers regarding potential fees and timescales for gaining permission. However, with scalability of services already an issue, TLSS need to consider to what extent they can task lecturers with clearing rights to use materials and how this is best supported.

Despite these issues, at the present time the existence of a dedicated team within Library Services demonstrates the valuable support for e-learning that a copyright clearance and scanning service can provide.

Scanning in the UK: results of a survey

In order to provide an overview of scanning activity in the UK this section presents results from a recent survey (Secker and Hedges, 2009). The survey provides a snapshot of activity relating to the digitization of core readings in higher education in the UK. Although this survey built on previous work carried out by SCONUL in 2007 and Delasalle (2007) there is relatively little written about scanning in UK academic libraries. In addition, any previous work looked at the impact of the CLA's Trial Licence which expired in 2008. This survey was deliberately launched shortly after the introduction of the CLA's Comprehensive Licence which permits higher education institutions to photocopy and scan from print published materials. However it also permits the copying of digital content, for example from e-books, e-journals or databases if institutions take out the full licence. The survey was launched in March 2009 and was widely publicized on mailing lists for universities involved in scanning material and dealing with copyright, for example the JISCmail list for HERON User Group members, but also LIS-Copyseek. It was a web-based survey and the results were collected and analysed using an online survey tool called Opinio, developed by the UCL.

Survey topics and response rate

The survey was designed to collect information about scanning under the CLA Licence in the UK, but also about operational decisions that were being made in university libraries to support this work. It covered the following areas:

◆ background and nature of institution
◆ digital readings at the institution
◆ copyright licensing and compliance, including the new CLA Licence
◆ procedural issues including scanning operations and delivery of readings
◆ management of readings
◆ wider issues such as collection management and how this work related to e-learning.

In total 44 institutions responded to the survey, although there were some gaps from larger universities. Of the respondents a disproportionate number were HERON members with 24 full HERON members completing the survey and three institutions who use the HERON software PackTracker replying. As HERON membership is approximately 50 of the 166 UK higher education institutions, this higher response rate from this group reflects the fact that the survey was promoted heavily at a HERON User Group meeting in December 2008. However the survey was not undertaken by HERON, but conducted independently by two librarians.

The respondents to the survey were mainly librarians, although a number of Copyright Officers (or CLA Licensing Coordinators) also responded. This reflects the fact that the vast majority of libraries are scanning published material to support e-learning, reflecting an expansion in the traditional role of library staff.

Digitization activities

The survey results demonstrate a clear increase in digitization activities in higher education, following the launch of the CLA Trial Digitization Licence in 2005 and its subsequent renewal in 2008. A blanket licence has advantages over the transactional licence that was expensive, difficult to budget and time-consuming to process. Very few libraries had a dedicated budget for copyright permissions, so where they were sought, permission fees were usually passed to academic departments or faculties. Transactional clearances were based on a 'per page per student' model, meaning the courses where there would be the greatest benefit in digitizing material (that is, where there were high student numbers) were extremely costly. Further details about the background to the move towards a blanket licence are discussed briefly earlier in this chapter and in more detail in Secker (2004, 7–10).

At the time of the survey all but one of the responding institutions had signed the CLA Licence, however only two institutions had signed the Comprehensive Licence covering 'born digital' material. More recent figures from January 2010 from the CLA show that the Licence has been signed by all 150 higher education institutions in the UK who are members of either Universities UK or Guild HE. Thirty-eight institutions had signed the Comprehensive Licence, and 122 had the Basic Licence. The CLA data also gives a more accurate picture of the amount of scanning undertaken by the sector as a whole, although at the time of publication the latest figures available were for 2007–8.

There is huge variation across higher education in the number of items that are scanned each year under the CLA Licence. For example the survey showed anywhere between 20 and 2844 readings were scanned in 2008–9, with a mean result of 515 scans. This figure is clearly skewed by the small number of institutions doing large amounts of scanning and consequently the median is considerably lower at 300. Most institutions were anticipating a growth in items they would scan in the next year and predicted a mean of 815 items with a median of 500. Data obtained from the CLA for the period 2007–8, show the mean number of scans across all institutions to be 341 digitized items per institution, suggesting the group who responded to the survey were more actively involved in scanning. However, compared to previous years, the mean number of scans has grown year on year since the licence was first launched in 2005. In 2005–6 just 46 scans were reported per institution and in 2006–7 this increased to 146. It seems likely that the 2008–9 figures from the CLA will confirm that the growth in scanning is continuing.

Staffing

Increasing numbers of UK libraries have established services to digitize core readings so this work is carried out centrally rather than devolved to academic departments. Early adopters of the approach to establish a centralized unit based in the library (notably, UCL, University of Sheffield, LSE and University of Derby) have been followed by others, although some exceptions do exist. Digitization teams have been set up in some institutions as part of the library's role in supporting teaching. Many institutions have a dedicated digitization team to ensure that records can be kept centrally. The survey found that there were variations in the number of staff involved in this work, with some institutions having no dedicated team and others having up to six full-time equivalent staff members. Of the respondents to the survey, 18 had a dedicated team while 19 did not. A third had seen an increase in staffing to cope with workload but the majority (25 respondents) had not and were redeploying staff from other areas to cope with the work at peak times of year. For example, in some institutions, teams who had processed paper course packs were redeployed to deal with digitization services.

Scanning readings

Scanning has become an increasingly straightforward process in terms of equipment required; however preparing copies suitable to distribution on the web does require a certain level of expertise. The survey therefore asked who undertook the scanning to establish if this was carried out in-house or outsourced. The survey found 17 institutions now carry out scanning in-house, with 6 saying that they would always outsource this work. Meanwhile 16 institutions engage in a mixture of both in-house and outsourced scanning (presumably dependent on timing, and the particular requirements in terms of quality).

Of the 29 respondents who said they outsourced either some or all of their scanning, the greatest number of institutions (14) used the Higher Education Scanning Service (HESS) provided by the British Library. The service was launched in 2008 as a solution for institutions that wanted to scan items under the CLA Licence but did not have internal facilities. Until this point the HERON service was the main service for outsourced scanning and 11 survey respondents were using HERON. Nevertheless, HERON membership has declined recently as the CLA Licence means that copyright clearance is not required for many UK and some overseas publications. Consequently many institutions are opting to undertake scanning in-house or using HESS. One area where HERON have acquired new customers recently is in the subscriptions to their rights management system, PackTracker. Fifteen of the survey respondents used PackTracker to manage the digitization process. This database has particular advantages as, in addition to helping manage the scanning process, it allows the CLA data report to be generated.

Scanned files are almost always provided to students in Adobe Acrobat PDF format. However, 13 respondents reported that they create text files using some form of optical character recognition (OCR) process. OCR technologies have also improved in quality significantly in recent years, becoming cheaper as well. Nevertheless 23 institutions reported that they did not produce text files and three institutions were not sure. Disability discrimination legislation in the UK has meant that an educational establishment should make appropriate adjustments for students with a disability. This could include providing readings in an accessible format that can be read by screen-reader software. Interestingly the survey asked whether institutions provided text files for visually impaired students and found that while 21 respondents did, ten did not and seven respondents again were unsure.

Managing demand for the service

The survey results suggested that managing demands for digitization services was a key issue for academic libraries. When asked whether they digitize all readings they were asked to by teaching staff the question generated the largest number of free text comments. These comments revealed that very few libraries have the capacity to digitize all of the items that are requested by teaching staff. Material that falls outside the CLA Licence is particularly problematic and a large proportion of libraries will only scan items that are covered by this Licence. Therefore, most libraries do not undertake copyright clearance work. However, some take a case-by-case approach, as this respondent stated: 'If the request falls outside the CLA Licence then a discussion is held with the academics as to whether we progress their request to the HERON service (at a cost to the department).'

Clearly the above library does not have an additional budget to pay for copyright permissions and these would need to be covered by the requesting academic department. Furthermore, a small number of institutions have an annual limit on digitization requests, either overall or per department or module. This limit can help libraries manage the scanning service and the consequent workload it creates. However, 84% of respondents did not have a limit on the number of requests a lecturer can place for scans. Managing demand for the service seemed to be done in other ways; for example 20% of respondents did not actively promote their services, relying instead on word of mouth. One respondent reported: 'We have been resistant to this [greater publicity] as we are unsure of demand and how we would cope.' Another stated: 'We have not really actively promoted it up to now because we have been trialling it and did not want to be overwhelmed.' These quotes are revealing, as some respondents acknowledged the need to scale up their services, but concerns over workload were more important, and ultimately prohibitive to expansion.

Delivery of readings: the role of e-learning

The CLA Licence requires that scanned readings are prepared for students on a course of study and only available behind password protection. However, the survey wanted to discover more about how electronic readings are delivered to students across higher education. The licence mentions the use of virtual learning environments but is not prescriptive about the method that a university uses to manage access to the material. Unsurprisingly, given the investment in e-learning from JISC, all institutions who responded to the survey reported that they had a VLE of some form and the majority of universities (36 out of 39) are using the VLE to deliver readings to students. However, VLEs are not the only option and 11 respondents are using a reading list system (some in conjunction with a VLE), one was using the Library catalogue (presumably with course level password protection in place) and four were using another method of delivery (a repository – again with some password protection).

In some instances library staff do not have access to the VLE, with nine of 39 respondents making this point. However, access to the VLE for library staff has improved dramatically recently, driven in part by the reporting element in the CLA Licence that has meant e-learning and library staff have had to work together more closely. Interestingly, in only four cases copyright permissions for other materials used in e-learning (such as multimedia content) were managed by the library.

While readings are delivered via the VLE, where they are stored was not always the same place and the survey revealed that readings tend to be stored either on a separate library server or in VLE although some institutions store scans in more than one place. The location of the scans is interesting as arguably material that is uploaded directly into an e-learning system then becomes difficult to trace from a copyright perspective.

Usage statistics

Libraries are often keen to collect statistics relating to the services they provide; however usage statistics about digitized readings were only collected by around a quarter of the survey respondents. Of those who did collect usage statistics, only three institutions actually acted upon them, for example not renewing requests if material was not used by students, or following up with a lecturer if the usage statistics far exceeded the number of students on a course. Several universities were aware that they should be collecting statistics and it seemed to be an area of concern for some librarians; for example one respondent stated: 'We would [take action based on usage stats] if we could get the stats from Blackboard – this is a sore topic!'

Interestingly only five respondents collect feedback on the digitization service in their library survey – either from staff who use the service or from students who access the readings. Again this demonstrated that more work could be done in this area.

Motivations for scanning

The survey asked institutions about the motives behind scanning core readings providing them with a choice of several motives and an 'other' option. The results showed that improving access to course readings was the most compelling reason for scanning a copyright work, cited by 37 respondents, with support for e-learning coming a close second (listed by 31 respondents).

To a lesser degree meeting student expectations was also a factor and cited by 22 respondents. Space and cost efficiencies were lesser still reasons with reducing the need for multiple copies (saving space) being mentioned by 13 respondents and reducing the need for purchasing multiple copies (to save money) being cited by only eight. Finally, raising the profile of the library was the lowest priority being mentioned by only six institutions. These findings are unsurprising and demonstrate that easy access to full text readings, often as part of the online support provided in the VLE, is a common expectation amongst students in higher education. With increasing numbers of e-books to supplement widespread availability of e-journals, the need to visit the library to get core readings is becoming less pressing. Therefore, the CLA Licence is in many ways ensuring that copyright content not yet available in electronic format is still read by students. The data supplied by universities to the CLA could also be used by publishers to inform their digitization programmes, although there is no evidence that this is happening. For the time being tutors all too frequently complain that without the inclusion of scanned published content in the VLE, students will simply read the easiest material to find through an internet search engine.

The HEI's relationship with CLA

The CLA website needs to be consulted regularly by library staff and teachers who are wishing to copy material, to check for exclusions to the repertoire. Perhaps unsurprisingly most respondents, who were librarians, reported that they did regularly consult the CLA website (76%). Interestingly institutions were lukewarm about the usefulness of this website with 65% (20 institutions) of respondents responding that it was 'quite useful' (only three people said they found it very useful and the remainder were indifferent). Anecdotal evidence also suggests that the frequent reorganization of this website is problematic to universities, who like to include links for teachers to documents such as the User Guidelines for the HE licence and the excluded works list.

The CLA Licence has specific reporting requirements for the higher education sector that means that bibliographic details of every item that is either scanned or used in digital format must be submitted on spreadsheet to the CLA annually, along with details of the course of study and the student numbers. The survey found that 15 institutions were using the HERON digitization management system, PackTracker, to manage the data reporting process. Twenty institutions were using the central record sheet that is supplied by the CLA. Meanwhile one institution asked academic departments to complete the record sheet and two institutions reported that they were using another method. In late 2008 the CLA established two working groups to help them better understand the needs of higher education. One working group is considering Data Reporting and Surveys, while the other is exploring the issue of the impact of the licence on textbook publishing. These working groups report to the CLA/Universities UK and Guild HE Copyright Group, which negotiates the licence for the entire sector. The working groups also reflect the CLA's desire to resolve issues of concern for publishers and for higher education.

Licence coverage

When the CLA Licence was launched in 2008 the repertoire included only UK publishers, with a separate list of excluded works. Since this date the licence has been extended to include some US publishers and most recently several other countries such as South Africa, Canada and Spain. At the time of the survey almost all respondents (31 out of 34) said they would like to see the repertoire increased further. Countries suggested, in order of frequency, include: all European countries, Australia, Netherlands, Germany, Ireland, Canada and Scandinavia. In addition, other countries or regions that were mentioned just once each included: the Far East, Japan, France, Spain, South Africa and one respondent asked for 'All English-speaking countries'.

One particularly problematic aspect of the UK licence is that currently the repertoire for photocopying is different to that negotiated for scanning and also for using existing digital content. This means that explaining the licence to teachers is complex and many do not understand why, for example, a particular title could be photocopied for their students but not scanned.

Handling copyright issues

Prior to 2005 when the first blanket licence for scanning was introduced, some universities sought permission to scan published works either through the CLA, the Copyright Clearance Center in the US or directly with publishers. Most, however, were using the HERON service to negotiate the permission on their behalf, although some institutions did process permission requests in-house. The survey was interested in finding out whether universities would still consider getting copyright permission for a core reading if it fell outside of the blanket licence. In fact the responses suggested that the majority of institutions do still seek copyright permission. Approximately 20% of the respondents stated that they would never get copyright permission to use material; however, the remainder did, with some using HERON (16), some applying directing to publishers (16) and some going to the Copyright Clearance Center (10) in the US.

The survey also explored how copyright was dealt with internally in universities and found that, of the responding institutions, 24 have a Copyright Officer, 13 do not and one respondent wasn't sure. Getting advice about copyright matters was often a concern for institutions, particularly where they did not have a dedicated Copyright Officer. However the survey found that the JISCmail list LIS-Copyseek was used most frequently for copyright queries, by 35 of the 38 institutions. To a lesser degree the CLA were consulted with queries (29), other colleagues at their institution were also a good source of advice (26) and where they existed, the institutional Copyright Officer (12) was of course important. These results are also particularly revealing given that many people who responded to this survey were the perceived copyright experts in their institution and often the person that academics and teachers in an institution would consult for copyright advice.

Collection management and e-resources

The final section of the survey explored the impact that digitization might be having on the collection management policies in academic libraries and the acquisition of electronic resources. Seventy-four per cent of respondents said that their collection management policy took into account the availability of e-books. Similar numbers of survey respondents would also check e-book availability before scanning an item. This finding is linked to one of the terms of the CLA Licence, which stipulates that institutions should check whether an electronic version of a published work is available before undertaking scanning. Publishers have been keen to stress that the licence should not be used to substitute primary sales, therefore if an institution takes the decision to scan an e-book or e-journal this is indicated on the CLA data return. The institution also needs to include the reason for scanning an item in place of purchasing the electronic text. In fact, purchasing single e-book titles can be problematic for libraries as many come in bundled deals, and thus, unsurprisingly, 23 respondents said that they might scan an e-book if they received a request from a teacher. Similarly some e-books are in a format that makes them unsuitable for distribution on an e-learning platform. In contrast, only three respondents claimed that they would scan a journal that was available electronically. In term of purchasing e-journals, there has been a greater flexibility in terms of buying single titles, which has only recently been possible with e-books. There are also a far greater number of electronic journals available while e-books are still having only a limited impact on academic libraries. Perhaps unsurprisingly almost all respondents said that electronic availability was having an impact on the paper collections in their Library.

Further issues

A variety of other issues were raised in the final open question at the end of the survey. Clearly the CLA Licence has shaped how UK academic libraries have established and managed digitization services. Common themes from the survey included complaints about the increase in workload for library staff, as more scanning is requested by teachers. For example, one respondent said: 'Managing digital readings is demanding, and requires extra staffing to do it properly.' Another commented: 'The issues of time, ongoing funding, difficulty of CLA reporting and problems of copyright compliance come up time and again.'

Almost all of the institutions mentioned the addition of the US publishers to the CLA Licence repertoire (in August 2008) as having had a major impact on their work. They were pleased that the remit of the licence had been extended and a few institutions noted that savings were being made due to them no longer needing to copyright-clear items; however this tended to be in those universities that had long established scanning services. Many institutions were generally concerned that managing the licence and renewing readings each year was generating extra work, as this respondent said: 'All these problems are exacerbated by up-scaling of each library's digitization service – even if there is not a concerted effort to increase through-put, just reusing items year on year means the time, reporting and staffing burdens are always increasing.'

Using published content outside of the UK

The results of the survey discussed above are only partial, yet they demonstrate that in the UK, licensing agreements and copyright has shaped the services offered by libraries to support e-learning. Digitization of core readings has gone from being a niche activity undertaken by larger institutions with established copyright clearance units, to a mainstream activity in academic libraries. Yet copyright and digitization work remains an activity that rarely is supported by a dedicated team. The work often falls between the remit of subject librarians and those in teaching support roles. It is rarely evaluated and very few procedures measuring performance are in place. The requirement to provide annual reports of materials digitized under the Licence is regarded by many as a hindrance to scaling up these services. Therefore, we see that, in the UK, copyright concerns rather than good pedagogic design are often shaping the nature of the e-learning content that is delivered to students. There is a real concern in UK libraries that VLEs need to be copyright compliant. While librarians are keen to use blanket licences to meet student demands, very few institutions have the resources to provide a scalable service. Many librarians in the UK are working hard to ensure that lecturers are aware of copyright issues and this means at times that they are perceived as being a barrier to e-learning.

Chapter 1 showed how many of the English-speaking countries of the world have followed the UK's example and the reprographic reproduction agencies in Australia, New Zealand and Ireland (to name but a few) now offer digitization licences. We have also seen that many countries in the world are attempting to reform their copyright laws, yet in most of the world using published content for education and specifically for online learning will require either negotiating individual permissions or taking out a blanket licence of some form. It will also inevitably mean that at times lecturers cannot add the resources that their students need to the VLE.

The USA

We have seen in Chapter 1 how the copyright laws in the United States are different to those in the UK and that this has impacted on the way in which published content is used in e-learning. The 'fair use' concept covers the copying of material for educational purposes, which means that, unlike elsewhere in the world, educational establishments have been able to make paper and digital copies for students for teaching purposes. Some institutions choose to seek copyright permission for material that was kept on electronic reserves for a long period of time, but many did not. However, in 2007 the US Copyright Clearance Center offered universities the option to take out a blanket licence. Opinions have been divided over the wisdom of purchasing such a licence, with some institutions seeing it as security and others feeling that it compromises the fair use provision. There follows a case study from a US university to contrast with the case study from the UK provided earlier in this chapter.

Case Study 3: Electronic reserves and copyright in a US university

Introduction and background

This case study is from a medium-sized liberal arts university in the eastern

United States enrolling approximately 5000 undergraduate and 2000 graduate students. Undergraduates fulfil general education requirements, choose a variety of elective courses, and pursue departmental concentrations and interdisciplinary certificate programs. At the graduate level students may earn advanced degrees in the humanities, social sciences, natural sciences and engineering.

To support the educational curriculum the Library has always offered a course reserve service to faculty. Faculty members would submit their requests for books, course packets or journal articles to be placed on reserve for their courses and staff would make them available to students through our closed reserve stack operation. Although the Library were certainly mindful of the copyright implications of duplicating journal articles, it was rare that they had more than two or three copies of the same article on reserve at any given time. The number of copies on reserve was determined by the numbers enrolled on the course. Most of the articles were from the Library's own collection to which, of course, the students had access and could make their own copies. Faculty members also had – and used – the option of having course packs created. These packs were created by an independent agency (for example, Kinko's), who would seek copyright permission to create the packs and pass any associated costs on to the students via the fee they charged. Because of the expense of these packs, faculty members would often supply one copy of the pack to be placed on reserve for student use.

The electronic reserves service

The Library began an electronic reserve service in 2001 as a pilot programme using courses in the humanities and social sciences. At that time they agreed to scan only journal articles and book chapters and adhered to the guidelines that were set at the Conference on Fair Use (CONFU). These guidelines suggested that scans should be limited to no more than 10% of a book or a single article from a journal issue. A small number of faculty members agreed to use the services in their courses during this pilot phase. Of course, for these and all other courses, the Library maintained a traditional course reserve operations. At the end of the pilot an assessment was conducted and, based on the positive feedback, the programme was expanded to all courses. Although the Library offers this service to all faculty members in all departments, not everyone was eager to take advantage of this new service. The popularity of service among the students however, helps to win some of the faculty members over in using electronic reserves. Some faculty members no longer saw the need for course packs since the same material was now being made available electronically to the students – and at no cost to them.

At the time, there was no commercially available product that managed electronic reserves processing. The integrated library system that the Library used, Voyager, did have an e-reserve component but it lacked many features including perhaps most importantly one that would restrict access to e-reserve readings only to students enrolled on a particular course. The locally developed system included an online request service for faculty members to submit the citations, as well as a complex database structure on the backend to manage those requests and to make the readings available. In addition to providing access via the Library's website using course-specific IDs and passwords, working with the University's IT department, staff were able to make the readings available through our course management system or VLE – Blackboard. Library staff encourage all faculty members who use the service to instruct students to access the e-reserve readings exclusively through Blackboard; reused access through the Library's website should be secondary and only if Blackboard was unavailable for some reason, or if someone in the course, such as an auditor, was unable to login via Blackboard.

Copyright compliance

Although the Library were fairly certain that they maintained copyright compliance by offering the electronic reserve service in a manner similar to our traditional reserve services, they consulted extensively with the campus' Office of General Counsel to ensure this compliance. Because they adhere to the CONFU guidelines, the Office felt that there was no need for further action at that time. For any item exceeding the guidelines set by CONFU the Library would seek permission from the copyright holder before making the item available to the students.

Using audio and video materials

Shortly after the success of the pilot and the more widespread implementation of the electronic reserve service, faculty members in the music department began asking how students could access the audio resources they needed for their courses. Working with the faculty and the IT department, library staff devised a system to record the audio material required, place it on a streaming server which is locally hosted, and make it available to the students from a resort location (the Library) and through a password-protected mechanism. As with the digitized printed items, the digitized audio items are available only to students enrolled in the courses for which those materials are needed.

Within the past four years the Library has seen an increase in the number of faculty members who are using video resources in their courses. Some disciplines, such as a film studies department, used these resources extensively in the past but faculty members in other departments now see the value in emphasizing points, making comparisons, or demonstrating effects of events through the use of video – both documentary and feature films. As a result, the Library which, until about five years ago, had a very small video collection has seen the size of the collection grow exponentially. Because of their positive experiences with both the digitized print and audio resources, faculty members using video resources also want a way to make these available electronically. Having had the experience with the audio reserves we used a similar model to present the digitized videos. As with the audio the Library digitize only content that they own in physical form (in this case either in Video Home System [VHS] or Digital Versatile Disc [DVD]) and it is made available only in streaming format, at select locations (in classrooms, in the library, and in the Video Resources Center), and restricted only to students enrolled on the courses for which the resources have been requested.

Conclusion

The Library believe that our electronic reserve services have been successful based both on the feedback that they have received from faculty and students and from the increasing number of requests for electronic reserve materials from the faculty members. They have also consulted extensively with our Office of General Counsel (OGC) to ensure that they are compliant. The OGC believes that the institution – and other libraries – should push the limits of fair use in order to protect those rights. The Library has not been pushing extremely hard but does push with strength sufficient to ensure that the resources that the faculty and students need are available to them in a format which is easy to access. As the number of court cases seems to be on the rise against those who use audio and video resources illegally, the Library has been more concerned about these operations than they are with the more traditional e-reserve service. However, because of the restrictions that the institution has in place (restricting access to certain locations, only to students enrolled on courses, and only to material that is physically owned) the OGC believes that they are in good stead. Naturally the Library keeps abreast of cases that could impact on operations, such as the case at the Georgia State University system and others that have been settled before reaching trial. The Library certainly hopes not to be in their company but continues to learn a lot from the experiences of others.

Using unpublished content

Unpublished content includes all manner of materials, such as theses, archival materials including letters, files and other historical materials. While it may seem out of place to discuss the use of unpublished material in this chapter, in fact there are many similarities to the copyright clearance process. In the case of unpublished content the author needs to be traced before a work can be digitized. Blanket licensing does not cover unpublished materials and therefore direct permissions need to be sought. Where the copyright owner can be traced it is sensible to keep records of any permission fees and the terms and conditions that the owner might have stipulated. Further details about requesting copyright permission for materials is available in Chapter 3 (see pages 67–8). When requesting copyright permission, always specify what you intend to do with the material, and include details such as:

◆ Who will have access to the material. If specific students on a course, specify student numbers and duration of permission required.
◆ What file format the material will be made available in, for example, PDF.
◆ If any password protection will be in place or if permission is sought to include it in an open access repository.

If a work is considered out of copyright than it can be digitized. In the United States some works are considered to be in the public domain and unrestricted copying can be undertaken. However, what is more problematic is when a rights holder cannot be traced despite reasonable endeavours. These works are often called 'orphan works' and if a teacher wants to go ahead and use an 'orphan work' then the institution needs to consider the risk of digitizing an item without permission. Questions to ask include:

- Is the owner likely to find out and object to the use of the material?
- Is the owner likely to be financially affected by the decision to digitize?
- Is the material sensitive in any way – are there any privacy or data protection issues?
- What would the institution be prepared to pay if the owner came forward?

Many UK universities have adopted a risk adverse approach to digitizing content without permission, concentrating on special collections that are either owned by an institution or material that is clearly out of copyright. Other material, which perhaps might be more useful for teachers, has tended to remain in archives in its original format. The possibility that orphan works might be reconsidered in the Digital Economy Bill would greatly reduce the problems that these items cause to libraries and archives. It might also mean that more unpublished works could be used in e-learning without concerns about copyright.

Conclusion

Institutions embarking on creating e-learning courses need to consider carefully how important the inclusion of published content might be. They will then need to ensure that they are familiar with the law and any licensing schemes in operation in their own country. There may be exceptions that allow published material to be scanned, but more often than not permission fees will need to be paid. This chapter has looked in detail at one country, the UK, where a licensing scheme has in many ways allowed published content to be used in e-learning. However, the survey shows that universities in the UK are not entirely happy with the terms of the licence and many still need to obtain copyright permission for material not covered by the licence. There are also many concerns about copyright issues and how scalable digitization services are provided. Meanwhile in the US 'fair use' allows limited amounts of published content to be scanned for educational purposes. However, publishers are extremely sensitive to any allegations of copyright infringement, or activities that may impact on their primary sales. Therefore, caution is advised when using any published content in e-learning. Course managers should ideally ensure that they have an adequate budget to pay for any necessary permissions if published content is required. Even using unpublished material is not without pitfalls and may require permission to be sought. High profile e-learning ventures by established universities mean that education is no longer seen as an entirely non-commercial enterprise. Consequently, if there is money to be made, many publishers, quite justifiably, would like to see some form of remuneration. Those involved in designing online courses need to be mindful of this when deciding what content they wish to include. Educational establishments also need robust copyright procedures in place to operate in this increasingly complex environment.

References

Copyright Licensing Agency (CLA) (2009a) *Key Dates in the History of the CLA*,
www.cla.co.uk/governance/cla_history [accessed 12 February 2010].

Copyright Licensing Agency (2009b) *Higher Education Licences*,
www.cla.co.uk/licences/licences_available/he/ [accessed 10 January 2010].

Delasalle, J. (2007) The CLA HE Trial Scanning Licence – how we're using it, *Library and Information Research*, 31 (98),
www.lirg.org.uk/lir/ojs/index.php/lir/article/view/39/46 [accessed 10 January 2010].

Secker, J. (2004) *Electronic Resources in the Virtual Learning Environment: a guide for librarians*, Chandos Publishing.

Secker, J. and Hedges, J. (2009) Digitisation of Core Readings Survey,
http://clt.lse.ac.uk/Projects/Digitisation_survey.php [accessed 10 January 2010].

3

Using multimedia in e-learning

Introduction

There is a growing demand for multimedia content, including images, video and audio materials, to provide engaging materials for use in both traditional teaching and in e-learning. However, copyright issues become increasingly complex when education professionals wish to digitize existing multimedia content. Obtaining permission to convert analogue recordings can be a complicated and expensive process. Meanwhile, producing multimedia content in-house is now technically straightforward but can raise a host of copyright issues. In both cases delivering multimedia content using an e-learning platform highlights, but also exacerbates, the copyright issues. This chapter will first explore the copyright issues associated with the digitization of multimedia, such as video and audio. In the UK, the Education Recording Agency (ERA) Licence permits broadcasts to be recorded 'off-air' and digitized for educational use. With several restrictions, this licence allows institutions to deliver this content via virtual learning environments. Elsewhere in the world there are other provisions under copyright laws that permit multimedia content to be digitized, but the situation is more complex. Second the chapter will consider digitizing commercially available multimedia material, for example recordings that can be purchased for educational use. Often in these situations permission is required from the rights holder and therefore the procedures for identifying the owner and for securing copyright permission are outlined.

Many educational institutions are now producing multimedia content in-house and there are a host of copyright issues that need to be considered.

For example, large-scale lecture capture systems are being installed in some universities in the United States, the UK and other countries. These offer institutions the possibility of recording and then delivering lecture material via a computer network. However, copyright issues are immediately more pertinent when classroom teaching is recorded and made available online. Aside from the need to get permission to include third-party content, the ownership of the resulting video also raises wider IPR issues in institutions. In some institutions teaching staff are raising concerns over their lectures being recorded and citing IPR issues. Third, this chapter explores some of these issues, including advice for dealing with third-party content and guidance for resolving the ownership of the resulting material. Finally the chapter includes a list of multimedia resources for teachers including sound, video and image collections that can be used for educational purposes without the payment of fees. Arguably, directing teachers to collections licensed for educational use is an important role for e-learning professionals. In doing this, knowledge about copyright issues becomes part of good practice in terms of finding and using resources for teaching. Sources of advice for resolving multimedia queries are also included. The case study in this chapter comes from the University of Oxford, who are delivering podcasts (video and audio) via the iTunes platform to students and the wider world.

Why use multimedia in teaching?

Multimedia is increasingly used in the classroom as a way of engaging students. Many authors have written about the changing way that students and young people find and use information and the relationship to learning. Concepts such as the 'Google' or 'Net Generation' were discussed briefly in Chapter 1 (see page 6). Whether you subscribe to Prensky's (2001) idea of young people being 'digital natives' in contrast to the 'digital immigrant' or agree with the notion of this generation of young people being somehow different, it is fair to say that young people have become increasingly visual learners. They are bombarded with music, moving and still images and consequently both audio and video resources are being used to enliven more traditional text-based teaching resources. These resources are a valuable way of conveying information to students who in the 21st century tend to spend more time watching television, playing computer games and using their mobile phones than they do reading books. There is also some evidence that using multiple media aids retention as it engages both aural and visual senses and caters to students with different learning styles. The use of audio and visual material to engage students is often a supplement to more traditional teaching methods, thus it is unsurprising that there is a growing demand by teachers to use this type of content in online learning.

Copyright and multimedia works: an introduction

Multimedia presents a whole set of copyright challenges for the e-learning professional. Multimedia also presents challenges for the copyright advisor who might be seeking to obtain permission for the reuse of content or advising over ownership of resulting materials. Establishing copyright ownership and obtaining permission to reuse printed materials such as books and journals are relatively well established processes, with many larger publishers having dedicated rights and permissions departments to handle requests. However, multimedia, be it sound, image or moving images has inherent problems as invariably the content is produced by more than one person. In addition there is no obvious body such as the Copyright Licensing Agency who can grant permission or act as a broker for handling permissions.

Copyright laws specify that format has an impact on the copyright protection that is offered to materials. So for example, the extent of copyright protection for sound and moving images is different in terms of the number of years that protection lasts. For example in the UK sound recordings are protected for 50 years from the year of creation, while films are protected for 70 years after the last to die of the principal director, author of the screenplay, author of the dialogue and composer of the music. This can mean in reality very few films are in fact out of copyright. Moreover film companies have been quick to extend copyright protection by re-issuing films. In the United States, sound recordings produced before 1978 are protected for 50 years but for those published after 1978 they qualify for 70 years' protection.

Copyright also becomes complicated when dealing with film, sound recordings and images as multiple copyright works are created. For example, performing a work such as a play is the exclusive right of the copyright holder and the performance can itself qualify for copyright protection if it is recorded. Performances qualify for protection for 50 years, as do broadcasts. Fair dealing is also a problematic area in relation to multimedia, for the exceptions apply to film and video and only include non-commercial research or private study, reporting current events and criticism and review. In relation to educational use, while they can be shown in the classroom for educational purposes, copying of films is prohibited except for training in film or film soundtrack production.

Digitization of analogue recordings

In the same way that print resources are digitized to improve access in the online environment, many institutions have started to invest in digitizing audio and video collections that were traditionally available in an analogue format. In the home entertainment market, video-recordings on VHS format have largely been superseded by DVD. Yet many libraries have been left with significant collections either on video or audio cassette. These collections are often under-used; they can be borrowed by individuals or shown in classrooms. However, a real advantage in terms of access could be made if the content was digitized and placed onto a streaming server that would allow delivery over a network. Digitization also facilitates the material being used in e-learning.

Format shifting to convert material from analogue to digital has become a relatively straightforward technical process. However, it raises all sorts of IPR issues, particularly if the intention is to place the digital file onto a network for educational use. Even when audio or video material exists in digital format (on CD or on DVD) the file format particularly of video material is often not suitable for delivery over a network without some processing. In addition, recordings such as videos, DVDs and audio CDs tend to be licensed for personal use only. We have seen in Chapter 1 how the Gowers Review recommended that format shifting for preservation purposes should be permitted under UK law. However, as yet this is not the case and therefore any format shifting of multimedia or distribution via a network requires negotiating a separate permission.

It seems relatively uncommon in the UK higher education sector for permissions to be sought to digitize multimedia such as commercial films or videos, or sound recordings. The perception amongst staff is that the process is both time-consuming and expensive, and experience at the LSE suggests that this may well be the case. It is frequently difficult to know who to approach to secure a permission to use an excerpt from a film – with copyright lying with several different individuals and largely being handled by a large multinational organization such as a film distributor. Getting permission from smaller educational companies can often be more straightforward, and surprisingly inexpensive. However, it is generally an area that, without a Copyright Officer, it is unclear who should be negotiating the permission (the academic, the e-learning team or perhaps library staff) and who should retain the documentation relating to the permission. Few universities are in the fortunate situation of the Open University to have a rights and permissions department that is well versed in negotiating permissions to use text, images and audiovisual materials in teaching.

Identifying rights holders and getting permission

If permission needs to be sought, the following guidelines can be used to help speed up the process and improve the chances of obtaining a positive response. This advice applies for other types of content not just multimedia. Sample letters for requesting copyright permission for materials are available in Secker (2004, 163–9). In order to obtain copyright permission take the following steps:

◆ First establish exactly what the teacher wants to do with the material, how much they wish to include (including exact timings of frames) and for what purpose. This will help establish if permission is required.
◆ Check what sort of budget might be in place to pay for any permission – is there a limit the teacher is prepared to pay?
◆ Spend some time establishing who owns the copyright of the material – check the copyright statement on any packaging or in the credits on a recording.
◆ Spend some time researching the organization or person ideally to trace a contact e-mail address. If they have a rights and permissions department approach them first.
◆ Send permission requests in written format (either by letter or e-mail)

or by following any specific instructions on the rights owners' web pages.

◆ Provide as much detail as possible about what you want to do with the material – for example what file format you will distribute the material in, what sort of password protection will be in place and most importantly who wants to access the material (student numbers) and for how long.

◆ Finally you may well need to send several reminders if you do not get a response to your message. Do not assume if you don't receive a response that you can go ahead.

◆ Ensure you keep teaching staff informed about the progress of their request.

◆ If permission is granted to use the material ensure that records are kept to manage the permission from year to year. If a licence is for a limited period of time ensure that teachers are aware of this restriction.

Copying broadcasts: The ERA Licence, www.era.org.uk

The UK Copyright, Designs and Patents Act 1988 permits recording of TV and radio broadcasts for educational use, but states that if a licensing scheme is available copying must be done in accordance with this. The Educational Recording Agency (ERA) Licence is available to educational establishments in the UK and covers scheduled free-to-air broadcasts on the following channels:

◆ BBC television and radio
◆ ITV Network services (including ITV2, ITV3 and ITV4)
◆ Channel 4, E4, More4 and Film4
◆ Five Television
◆ S4C.

Recording of off-air broadcasts must be undertaken in accordance with the terms of this licensing scheme, rather than under any exceptions in UK copyright law. However, the ERA Licence is relatively permissive and allows educational establishments not only to record broadcast output, but also to copy this material. Furthermore, it does not specify the nature of the recording, for example analogue versus digital. Recordings can take place within the establishment or off the premises, for example they can be undertaken by a lecturer at home. The licence specifies that recordings must be labelled appropriately to include the name, time and date of the broadcast. Recordings can be shown in the classroom or elsewhere on the premises of the educational establishment; they can also be deposited in the library to facilitate access to the material by students.

There are limits to the ERA Licence; for example it does not cover on-demand television services, nor does it cover Open University broadcasts, which have a separate licensing scheme. It also prohibits recordings being accessed outside the educational establishment. In other words, if uploading to a VLE the institution needs to have a security system in place that restricts access to the premises only. Problems arise because the ERA Licence also does not have jurisdiction outside of the UK, and so access to the material by students based outside of the UK, for example distance learners on an e-learning course, is prohibited. In 2007 ERA launched a new licence called ERA+ which was reported to allow distance learners to access recordings. Unfortunately this licence still requires a blocking of access to recordings outside of the UK, which has led many institutions to question its value and not take out this additional licence. Finally, satellite and cable broadcasts are not covered by the ERA Licence, however because a licensing scheme for this material is not available, educational establishments are currently free to copy this material under the exceptions in UK copyright law, provided the material is free-to-air and not from an encrypted or subscription service. Premium rate satellite and cable channels such as Sky Movies are not covered by this exception.

There have also been some interesting developments to enhance the services provided to universities by the British Universities Film & Video Council (BUFVC) to support e-learning. This organization provides a number of services to universities, for example the recording back-up service, where using a database known as TRILT (Television and Radio Index for Learning and Teaching http://bufvc.ac.uk/tvandradio/trilt) you can find out when a programme was broadcast and request an off-air recording. BUFVC also run numerous training courses in the area of digital media production and a one-day course focusing on obtaining copyright for multimedia resources. Further details are listed in the Conclusion on pages 190–2.

Box of Broadcasts, http://bobnational.net

Another service available to UK further and higher education is Box of Broadcasts (BoB) which is an off-air recording and media archive service. BoB is only available to institutions who are members of the British Universities Film & Video Council and who hold an ERA+ licence. It is a TV scheduling service which permits staff and students to record TV and radio programmes that are scheduled for broadcast during the next seven days. It is also possible to retrieve programmes from the last seven days from a selected list of recorded channels. After a programme is recorded, users receive a Flash video file that can be viewed in a web page. However, BoB also stores recorded TV and Radio programmes in an archive indefinitely which allows other users to access them. The archive offers many TV and radio programmes and will increase as a greater number of further and higher education institutions join BoB.

Catch up TV services/television on demand

The ERA Licence and copyright exceptions in the law are hugely valuable for using broadcast material in teaching in the UK; however they require using an 'off-air' recording. Meanwhile, many of the television channels are now making use of internet technologies to provide catch-up or 'listen again' services on their websites which is effectively a TV on demand service. However, with many of these services, television and radio programmes are not archived on the web in perpetuity and are only available for a relatively short period of time (such as seven days) after the original broadcast. Teaching staff frequently ask about the legality of using material from on-demand TV services such as the BBC iPlayer (www.bbc.co.uk/iplayer) or the ITV Player (www.itv.com/itvplayer). Under UK law TV on demand services such as the iPlayer are not defined as broadcast, and so the educational exceptions do not apply. In all cases we need to consider the licence agreements governing these services.

BBC iPlayer

In the case of the BBC, the iPlayer service is available for a week after a programme has been broadcast. Not all TV and radio broadcasts are available on the iPlayer, but the broadcasts can be watched via a streaming service, or downloaded onto a computer if you are based in the UK. Note that the download service is only available in the UK, and that downloaded files are encrypted with digital rights protection (DRP) that means they will be deleted from your computer after their expiry date. Any attempt to remove the DRM protection from a downloaded file would be illegal under UK (and other) laws.

The use of the BBC iPlayer is governed by Terms of Use, however under the frequently asked questions the BBC state that: 'Teachers are free to play radio programmes in BBC iPlayer to classes. The playing or performing of copyright works, including sound recordings, in the course of activities of educational establishments does not infringe copyright.'

For the short time that programmes (be they radio or TV broadcasts) are available they could, for one example, be added as a link from an e-learning system, or shown in the classroom. However, copies cannot be made of the streamed recordings.

Frequently asked questions and help are available about the BBC iPlayer at: http://iplayerhelp.external.bbc.co.uk.

Creating audio/video content in-house: copyright issues

Increasingly educational establishments are moving towards creating audio and video content in-house, partly to avoid the copyright issues associated with using commercial recordings or other third-party materials. While this requires an investment in terms of equipment and staff expertise to produce professional recordings, many universities are keen to capitalize on the expertise and knowledge of their teaching staff. University staff sometimes have press and broadcasting experience and some academics are regularly interviewed by newspaper, television and radio journalists when expert opinions are required. It could therefore be seen as sensible for universities to utilize this expertise to produce video and audio content both for their website to promote the institution, and for teaching purposes. Many larger universities host topical events and public lecture series that will have wider appeal if they are recorded and made available online. While the costs associated with producing this type of content are not insignificant, digital recording equipment has fallen dramatically in price recently, so that highly professional recordings can be made at a relatively low cost.

Aside from the technical skills and equipment requirements, legal issues, specifically copyright and other IPR issues, need to be considered when producing this material in-house. When recording individuals from outside of the institution it would be typical to ensure that they sign a release form, to make certain that they have given their consent for the resulting recording to be reused. In addition, it is vital that care is taken to ensure any third-party content is either removed from the video or appropriate permission is sought for its inclusion. For example, if a speaker is showing images, clips from videos or audio recordings in the lecture, permission will usually be required if the resulting material is going to be hosted on a network. A release form can be a useful way to remind people that permission may be needed for some of their content, if it is not entirely their own.

Institutions would be wise to use a release form so that they can claim copyright in the resulting production and reuse it where they see fit. Under employment law, if teachers or lecturers are recorded it would be standard practice that the institution would own this resulting material. However, some academic staff might question this decision and JISC recommended in 2006 that all universities should have an IPR policy to define this type of issue and provided further details in their report (JISC, 2006). IPR policies of several universities are listed in the Conclusion, for those institutions who are seeking to develop such a document.

Podcasting and audio recordings

Creating podcasts, audio recordings, lectures or public events is technically more straightforward than producing a video. It also can avoid the copyright issues associated with recording visual material, where it could be easy to inadvertently include images or other multimedia from third parties. Care still needs to be taken, however, to ensure that any audio played during a lecture and subsequently recorded (for example, any music) either has the appropriate licence or that copyright permission has been sought. A variety of equipment is now available to facilitate the creation of audio recording such as digital recorders, radio microphones and recording software embedded into e-learning. Commercial and open-source products are once again available; for example Wimba (www.wimba.com) offer a suite of tools including voice-recording facilities and online classrooms tools. As a performance, the lecture will qualify for copyright protection. Some institutions have an explicit statement to indicate that they (rather than the individual) will own the resulting podcast. Other institutions ask lecturers to sign a release form to grant them a licence to distribute the content. This is particularly useful if you are recording external speakers, as they should be explicitly told what the recording will be used for, who will own the resulting copy and where it will be placed. A release form can also be useful as it usually asks the lecturer to specify if their material includes any third-party content that might require copyright clearance.

Lecture capture and IPR issues

Lecture capture is the term used to describe the recording of a lecture. EDUCAUSE (2008), the US not-for-profit organization (discussed in more detail on page 188) define the term as 'any technology that allows instructors to record what happens in their classroom and deliver it digitally'. Until relatively recently lecture capture was usually restricted to an audio recording of the event, which might enable students to either revise or catch up on a missed lecture. Some universities routinely recorded lectures onto audio-cassette, for example if there was a clash in the timetable that might prevent groups of students from attending. However, in the last few years, increasing numbers of universities are investing in large scale lecture capture technology, which once installed in the classroom or lecture theatre, enables the entire lecture (audio, video and screen capture) to be recorded with fairly minimal intervention for technicians. The value of recording lectures has been recognized since the 1970s, however video-recording equipment has historically often been expensive and complex to use. In addition, few institutions could afford to employ dedicated audiovisual technicians to process this material. This meant that those institutions that were recording lectures were usually simply audio recording the lecture. However, arguably the development of products such as Echo360 (www.echo360.com) and Sonic Foundry's MediaSite (www.sonicfoundry.com) that are complete automated lecture capture systems, might have the potential to revolutionize the lecture experience.

Lecture capture or video-recording of lectures however raises several interesting copyright issues, including:

◆ the ownership of the resulting recorded lecture
◆ whether it can be shown if a lecturer subsequently leaves an institution
◆ how to deal with any third-party content that might be included in the lecture
◆ who might be responsible for any copyright infringement if third-party content is shown in the lecture.

The ownership of teaching materials in higher education has for many years relied on an unwritten agreement that respects academic and intellectual freedom. While a university as an employer might legally own the materials produced by their teaching staff under employment law, they would rarely assert this ownership. This is very different from a commercial organization that would regard the intellectual output of their staff as their property. However, classroom technologies such as lecture capture do concern some members of academic staff, and at the London School of Economics and Political Science currently lecture capture is undertaken only with the express permission of the teacher. The recordings are not routinely archived and used in subsequent years and staff are advised to seek permission or remove any third-party content from their lectures that are recorded. Those institutions investing in such technologies would be advised to ensure that they resolve IPR issues early on to avoid any potential misunderstandings or problems in this area.

Screen recording

Seen by some as part of the lecture capture process, there are a number of free commercial screen-recording tools available which allow instructors to create educational videos for their students. Commercial software includes products such as Camtasia Studio and Adobe Captivate. Meanwhile free or open-source tools include CamStudio, ScreenToaster, Jing, Wink and Webinaria.

There are several copyright issues to be aware of when creating screen recordings, particularly if you wish to create demonstrations of other software. However, in general the same advice applies to creating any multimedia in-house and where possible, to avoid using any third-party materials without clearing the rights. It is also advisable to check the licence of specific software if you wish to make a screen recording which includes a named product. For example, if you were creating a screen recording to demonstrate how to use the reference management software Endnote then you should check the Endnote licence to ensure that this is covered.

iTunes U, www.apple.com/education/mobile-learning

The iPod and other MP3 players, many of which are now integral to mobile phones, have revolutionized the way in which many people buy and listen to music and other audio content. Increasingly mobile devices also allow digital video to be viewed. In recognition of the growing demand for 'mobile learning' Apple launched iTunes U in May 2007 in partnership with Stanford University, UC Berkeley, Duke University and MIT. The service manages, distributes, and controls access to educational audio and video content for students within a university as well as on the wider internet. Content is free to users, although password restrictions may apply to manage access to certain content within an institution. It is now used by universities in the USA, United Kingdom, Australia, Canada, Ireland and New Zealand. The Member institutions have their own iTunes U site that makes use of Apple's iTunes Store infrastructure. Further information is available in Case Study 4 from the University of Oxford, who were the first university outside of the United States to go into partnership with Apple to provide audio and video-recordings available via the iTunes platform.

Case Study 4: Open educational resources, Oxford on iTunes U and OpenSpires, University of Oxford, UK

Melissa Highton, Peter Robinson, Rowan Wilson

Introduction

This case study describes the approach that the University of Oxford has taken to licensing podcast (audio and video) learning materials for widespread dissemination and reuse. There is a growing trend amongst educators to see open educational resources (OER) as a cost-effective, sustainable and global approach to making high quality digital resources available to support learning and teaching. When material is made available publicly online there are legal processes and procedures that the department and individual contributor must follow to ensure that the material is sensibly recorded, edited and released in a manner that meets the University's legal obligations. Success in this area is dependent on key parallel developments in Creative Commons licensing. Oxford University Computing Services worked closely with the University Legal Services Office to ensure that the institution can be flexible and adept in making materials available for reuse by learners and researchers in the wider community.

Background

In October 2008 Oxford University launched a new podcasting service using Apple's iTunes U software. The Oxford on iTunes U service (University of Oxford, 2010) offers a wealth of academic audiovisual material from across the collegiate University and is managed by Oxford University Computing Services (OUCS). OUCS is the University's primary computing infrastructure providing facilities such as the network backbone, central e-mail, web, news, backup servers and virtual learning environments, as well as supporting the effective use of IT in all disciplines.

All the material offered via iTunes U is free-to-download. The range of audio and video-recordings reflects the breadth of high quality teaching and research across the University. The service proved to be very popular, attracting a global audience of the intellectually curious who subscribed to, and downloaded, over two million items in just over a year.

In April 2009 the podcasting team began a new project to release a significant proportion of Oxford audio and video assets as open educational resources. This initiative was supported by the University senior management, by funding from the UK Joint Information Systems Committee and by the Higher Education Funding Council for England. The OpenSpires project focused on supporting strategic institutional learning and encouraging cultural change. The outcomes may inform and influence policy in other research-intensive institutions in the UK HE sector and beyond (JISC, 2009).

Open educational resources

Open Educational Resources are discussed briefly in Chapter 1. Well known university OER projects include the MIT OpenCourseWare Initiative (MIT, 2010), Carnegie Mellon University's Open Learning Initiative (Carnegie Mellon University, n.d.), and the African Virtual University (2010). Such initiatives aspire to provide open access to high-quality educational resources on a global scale. The current trend towards OER is primarily values driven. Openness is increasingly seen as a desirable practice. Figure 3.1 shows University of Oxford OER materials on the iTunes website.

Open content initiatives must overcome considerable barriers to reusing educational content. University intellectual property rights are complex in universities where there may be reluctance to 'give away' resources with potential value. Academic colleagues often have legitimate concerns over attribution, reputation and digital and academic identity. Moves towards making materials freely and openly available in digital form have required careful support work in learning technology services as well as changes and development in copyright licensing and law.

Figure 3.1 *University of Oxford OER materials on iTunes U*

Although the values and underpinnings of the OER movement are strong and the availability of open educational content is increasing, its use and reuse is still hampered by confusion and incompatibility of licences. Creating learning resources by drawing from a number of existing ones to create something new for a specific teaching context becomes a very complex task if the resources you are using come with different granted permissions. Although there are a number of different definitions of OER they all share some fundamental values; namely, that resources are licensed for unrestricted distribution and that there is the possibility of adaptation and improvement. Recently OER producers have begun to take a consistent approach to the use of licensing. CCLearn is a division of Creative Commons dedicated to realizing the full potential of the internet to support open learning and open educational resources.

The decision to grant a Creative Commons License to materials may lie with an institution, or it may lie with an individual. Where open educational resources have been commissioned under specific initiatives and projects, the ownership and intellectual property may be clearly located; where individual teachers and academics make these choices for themselves the decision making process may be more complex.

The openness challenge

University of Oxford IP policy required that for every podcast recorded, an agreement form from the podcast 'author' needed to be signed before it was made available. For the Oxford on iTunes U service the University's Legal Services Office (LSO) drafted agreements to be used to cover all podcasting-style activities. Apple required the University to make promises ('warranties') about the kind of content that would be in the podcasts (no copyright infringement, nothing defamatory or pornographic, and so forth), as well as requiring the granting of rights to the material (for example, the right for Apple to use excerpts in promotional material). Since Oxford podcast materials are generated, and owned, by the academic contributors, Oxford University, as such, could not grant those rights or make those promises for the material.

The solution reached in 2008 was that the iTunes U agreement between the University and the contributor should use almost exactly the same language as the agreement between Apple and the University. Since iTunes U has a very high public profile and therefore attracts more potentially litigious eyes (and ears) LSO resolved that there should be little difference between the 'inbound' language and the 'outbound' language. This reduced the University's risk to a minimum, brokering a grant of warranties and rights between the contributor and Apple.

In 2009, however, during the OpenSpires project, that licence was reviewed. The iTunes U licence asked for rights and warranties 'specifically in order to participate in the iTunes U project'. This meant that exercising the rights for other purposes was not allowable.

While iTunes U and OpenSpires were distinct projects, their sources of material are common. Ideally an Oxford contributor to iTunes U needed to be able to decide to Creative-Commons-license their material via OpenSpires at the same time as agreeing to the stipulations for the iTunes U distribution. While this could be done via two separate agreements, ideally this would all be encompassed in a single, relatively simple, agreement.

What was needed was a new assignment for a new OER programme of webcasting. This agreement – like the iTunes U one – asks the contributor to provide warranties that the material does not infringe the copyright of others and is not defamatory and so on but in contrast to the iTunes U agreement, asks the contributor to 'assign' (give) their rights in the material to the University. This enables the University to make much wider use of the material, possibly licensing it out themselves and using it for pretty much any purpose. The University then in turn gives the contributor a very wide licence back – meaning that they can do almost everything with the material that they could have done when they owned it. Figure 3.2 is an extract from draft University of Oxford OpenSpires recording release form.

[…]We would like to capture your presentation in audio and/or video and/or still photographs. To that end we want to make certain that both you and the University of Oxford have the necessary rights and protections to continue to benefit from your presentation. At the end of the process a copyright release in the form attached will be generated, covering the captured presentation (the ⊠Recording'). If you are uncertain of the copyright status of any of the materials you intend to use in the Recording, please provide a list of these materials so that together we may discuss the situation.

The University of Oxford will hold the copyright in the Recording and will distribute it under a Creative Commons UK: England & Wales licence of your choice. So, for example, the Recording might be made available with the following notice: *'Recording' by A. Scholar, Department of University, © University of Oxford [date]. This work is licensed under the Attribution-Non-Commercial-No Derivative Works 2.0 UK: England & Wales.*

[…]As a result of making the Recording available under a Creative Commons licence, others will be able to redistribute it provided they continue to attribute the work to its creator and copyright holder. Depending on which licence you choose, others may also be permitted to use the Recording for commercial purposes and incorporate segments of the Recording in other works.

Figure 3.2 *Extract from draft University of Oxford OpenSpires recording release form*

Conclusion

When Oxford University made a commitment to publish materials as OER we planned to easily adapt our existing processes for podcasting and publishing. After discovering that the contribution form created to facilitate the original iTunes U project did not encompass any other activities than release on iTunes U the project team generated a second form to cover wider reuse and release under Creative Commons for the OpenSpires initiative. Learning technologists and legal officers have been working hard with all parties concerned to create a unified form that suits both of these purposes, and is flexible enough to encompass future plans.

References

African Virtual University (2010) Home page,
www.avu.org/home.asp [accessed 12 February 2010].
Carnegie Mellon University (n.d.) Open Learning Initiative,
http://oli.web.cmu.edu/openlearning/ [accessed 12 February 2010].
JISC (2009) *Open Educational Resources Programme*,
www.jisc.ac.uk/oer (accessed 5 January 2010).
MIT (2010) OpenCourseWare Initiative,
http://ocw.mit.edu/ [accessed 12 February 2010].
Open University (n.d.) OpenLearn,
http://openlearn.open.ac.uk/ [12 February 2010].
University of Oxford (2010) The University of Oxford on iTunes U,
http://itunes.ox.ac.uk/ [accessed 12 February 2010].

Digital images collections

This section concentrates on dedicated image collections rather than incidental or illustrative images found on websites. Images are particularly useful in many educational subjects from science to art, history to medicine. They add interest to text-based content and in some cases may be a more appropriate way of conveying information. However, like audio and video material they can be problematic and the fair dealing exceptions do not apply to images.

Digital image collections fall into several categories including:

◆ Commercial or subscription collections that are available either on a pay per item basis or as a subscription for the collection. Examples of these include the Getty Image Archive, the Education Image Gallery, private image collections either from photographers, artists or art galleries and museums such as the Bridgeman Art Gallery.

◆ Image collections where the content is considered to be out of copyright or in the public domain. These are often made available by libraries, museums or other charitable bodies. Examples of these include collections from the University of Virginnia library, MorgueFile (www.morguefile.com), and Images of America.

◆ Image collections that have been licensed under Creative Commons Licenses and so can be reused under the terms of these licences. Flickr the photo-sharing website is the largest example of this type of collection and is discussed in more detail in Chapter 4.

◆ Other image collections which can be used for educational purposes, for example, FreeFoto (www.freefoto.com).

One of the issues of making digital images available in any online collection is that they are technically very easy to copy. Images are also problematic in terms of copyright laws because while small insubstantial parts of textual material can be copied under provisions such as 'fair dealing' or 'fair use' it is difficult to copy only part of an image. Those who copy or download images invariably copy them in their entirety as it is difficult to copy part of an image, so the copyright exception 'fair dealing' thus does not apply. Professional photographers and those such as art galleries who rely on their images for a revenue stream tend to protect their images in ways such as using watermarking, whereby the details of the copyright owners are clearly visible across a photo, limiting its use. Other rights protection techniques include making only low resolution files available online, with the higher resolution copies needing to be ordered for a fee.

Many subscription or commercial image collections tend to be governed by either license agreements or terms and conditions. These set out how the images can be used and usually specify how the images must be credited. Meanwhile, in the UK the Design and Artists Copyright Society (DACS) provide a range of licences for those wishing to copy artistic works.

One-off licences for copying specific material can be obtained and the pricing structure is fixed. Many universities teaching fine art use the DACS slide licence scheme to allow them to reproduce artistic works in lectures. DACS also have a reciprocal agreement with the CLA that allows artistic works within published works to be digitized under their higher education licence. These need to be recorded on the CLA record sheet so that payments can be returned to the artists in question. However, to date a DACS digital licence to replace the slide licence has yet to be issued. This would offer many advantages to those developing e-learning content, as it would allow universities to digitize their slide collections and integrate the materials into e-learning platforms.

Where licences are not available, UK copyright law is clear about copyright ownership of images. It states that:

◆ Images are protected as artistic works and copyright lies with the artist.
◆ Copyright of photographs taken after 1989 are owned by the person taking the photograph, even if the photograph is commissioned by another person.
◆ Commissioned artistic works pre-1989 are owned by the person commissioning the work.
◆ Copyright protects taking photographs of artistic works unless they are on permanent display and open to members of the public.
◆ Owners of artistic works (such as galleries and museums) may still charge a copying fee for a work in their possession – despite the work being out of copyright.

Anyone seeking permission to reproduce an artistic work is advised to consult DACS (www.dacs.ac.uk) in the first instance for further advice.

Managing multimedia content

While this is not strictly a copyright issue, managing multimedia content is increasingly an issue for institutions who are building up collections of digital media that they either own or have permission to distribute. Traditional library catalogues can provide bibliographic information about multimedia content but increasingly libraries have decided that digital files are often better managed in other systems. In other institutions digitization is undertaken by audiovisual units or e-learning teams so management of these resources may not have been considered a priority. Encouraged by funding bodies such as JISC, some universities in the UK have invested in building 'learning object repositories' which can effectively store multimedia content. Several commercial and open-source solutions are also available such as:

- Intralibrary (www.intrallect.com/index.php/intrallect/products)
- Drupal (http://drupal.org)
- Dspace (www.dspace.org)
- Eprints (www.eprints.org).

Traditional library system vendors also provide solutions for managing digital media files, such as:

- Ex-Libris Digitool
  (www.exlibrisgroup.com/category/DigiToolOverview)
- Serials Solutions product Summon
  (www.serialssolutions.com/summon).

In many instances the physical location of multimedia files remains a considerable issue because of the relatively large file size. In addition, many institutions are keen to provide this content in streamed format to facilitate access, rather than requiring individuals to download files in order to listen to or watch the content. Streamed files in general require storage on specialist servers and increasingly institutions require metadata to manage access to the material and storage space for the files. Metadata schema, such as Dublin Core, includes fields for describing rights information and it is vital that rights information is stored alongside digital media. So, for example, if material has been digitized with the permission of a commercial publisher, or is available under a licence, this information needs to be retained alongside the digital object. While many large educational institutions have resolved this issue through using a repository or specialist digital library tool, in small organizations where resources are more limited this is unlikely to be the case. Therefore, it is vital that records are retained and that a system is devised for managing licence or rights information alongside the digital files. This could take the form of a simple spreadsheet or database, which would then also facilitate reuse of the content. Whatever system is used it should ensure that if copyright permissions need to be renewed, alerts or reports can indicate this in good time, so that they are not overlooked.

Finding multimedia content for use in e-learning

There are many different collections of images, video and audio that are available for use in an educational context, some of which are free at the point of use. Other collections are subscription resources, where a licence fee is paid by the institution. In most cases institutional licences will then allow unlimited use of the material in the collection for teaching purposes. A selection of resources is provided in the next section, although this list is not comprehensive and is intended only to provide a starting point. It is recommended that e-learning teams draw up a list of resources that can be maintained in-house for teachers, to direct them to appropriate multimedia and image collections. The Centre for Learning Technology at London School of Economics and Political Science, maintain such a list for teaching staff, which is illustrated in Figure 3.3.

Figure 3.3 *LSE Centre for Learning Technology: Multimedia Resources page: http://clt.lse.ac.uk/Multimedia/ Multimedia-Resources.php*

It is always worth reminding teachers of Creative Commons Licenses that indicate when an author is happy to share their work. Staff should also be encouraged to use the Creative Commons website which can be searched to find resources. The Creative Commons Search is available at http://search.creativecommons.org.

The site does not actually brand itself as a search engine but rather links to the search engines of other websites; for example it searches the photo-sharing website Flickr for images. Those who wish to reuse resources they find through regular search engines will need to obtain copyright permission if the material is not licensed under Creative Commons or a similar scheme.

Example sources for still images

Cartoons for the classroom, http://nieonline.com/aaec/cftc.cfm

A selection of cartoons from the Association of American Editorial Cartoonists is available for use in teaching. Covering many of the major political events of the 20th century, these cartoons can be downloaded for use in the classroom.

Education Image Gallery (EIG), http://edina.ac.uk/eig

Higher and further education institutions can subscribe to the Education Image Gallery, a collection of thousands of images which have been selected for educational purposes at higher and further educational institutions. The collection is updated monthly and spans diverse subject areas such as architecture, archaeology, arts, culture and entertainment, environmental issues, industry, leisure, news, music and politics. All images are free to download for use in teaching and research and can be displayed online via a secure network, such as an e-learning system.

morgueFile, www.morguefile.com

Registration is only required if you want to submit photos; downloading and redistribution is allowed 'for . . . ordinary personal and/or commercial purposes'. You do not need to include credits with the photo. It is not clear how many images are available. The unusual name is a publishing term for a place to keep reference material.

Pics4Learning, www.pics4learning.com

A 'copyright-friendly' image library for teachers and students. The thousands of images in the collection are all donated by students, teachers and amateur photographers. Permission is granted for teachers and students to use the images in print, multimedia, and video productions, within an educational setting.

FreeFoto.com, www.freefoto.com/index.jsp

This is an archive of over 100,000 photos that are 'free to private non-commercial users'. However, there are conditions for educational use: students may use images in their own work, and teachers may use the images in 'their own personal teaching work'. However, permission is not given to distribute images outside of the classroom, so they cannot be used on websites. In all cases, images must be credited with '© Ian Britton – FreeFoto.com'.

Google Image search, http://images.google.com/advanced_image_search

Google now offers a 'licensing filter' for its image search, so you can search for images that you will be able to reuse in your teaching without needing to ask for permission. Note, however, that you may still need to attribute the work – check the specific licence that applies in each case to find out whether this is necessary.

Example sources for moving images

BFI InView, www.bfi.org.uk/inview

BFI InView is a collection of diverse and rarely seen moving image titles focusing on the changing social, political and economic landscape of Britain in the 20th and into the early 21st century. The content is searchable and also comprehensively catalogued and organized under seven main historical categories (education; health; environment; immigration; race and equality; industry and economy; and law and order). Sources include television documentaries, party political broadcasts, Parliamentary debates and newsreels. Please note that this is a subscription resource for higher and further educational institutions.

BFI Screenonline, www.screenonline.org.uk

This is an archive of information and clips from Britain's cinema and TV history. Most entries for films and programmes provide several streamed video clips.

blinkx, www.blinkx.com

blinkx is a video search engine that uses speech recognition and video analysis to filter its results. It claims to be the world's largest index of video content on the web, indexing over 35 million hours of video. The video content comes from a wide range of providers including national broadcasters and commercial media producers (such as the British Broadcasting Corporation [BBC], Home Box Office [HBO] and Music Television [MTV]). The videos available are for the most part streamed, so they may be linked to, but not downloaded.

British Pathe film archive, www.britishpathe.com

The British Pathé film archive contains over 3500 hours of British Pathé film footage, covering news, sport, social history and entertainment from 1896 to 1970. The still and moving image files are free to use, but for a UK audience only. The images/audio files can be presented in the classroom and/or within a password protected, online environment, such as Moodle.

iTunes U, www.apple.com/education/mobile-learning

iTunes U manages, distributes, and controls access to educational audio and video content for students within a university as well as on the wider internet. Content is free to users, although password restrictions may apply to manage access to certain content within an institution. It is now used by universities in the USA, United Kingdom, Australia, Canada, Ireland and New Zealand.

NewsFilm Online, www.nfo.ac.uk

NewsFilm Online is another service from Edina for further and higher education in the UK which is currently free until July 2012. It offers access to over 3000 clips from ITN and Reuters ranging from 1910 onwards. It is possible to link to and download clips to be made available through a virtual learning environment.

News on Screen from BUFVC, http://bufvc.ac.uk/newsonscreen

This database was formerly known as British Universities Newsreel Database and holds 160,000 records of British cinema newsreel production from 1910 to 1979 and a large collection of digitized documents. It is available to BUFVC members and once registered you can download film clips from various organizations, such as Pathé News. Please note that in some instances the database contains documentation about a film and not the actual film itself. Documentation can include original commentaries and shot lists.

Teacher Tube, www.teachertube.com

This site was launched in 2007 by a US teacher and is modelled on YouTube the video-sharing website, but aims to provide educational video content. It also contains images, audio and teaching resources. It has a search function and you can also browse the extensive list of channels. The content comes largely from school teachers, although some university level material is also available.

YouTube EDU, www.youtube.com/edu

Launched in March 2009, this popular video-sharing website now has an educational channel for sharing content from some of the world's leading universities who are using YouTube. It is an eclectic mix of lectures, interviews with Vice Chancellors and promotional materials. Universities need to apply to have their content available on this channel so there is some form of quality control.

Example sources for audio

British Library Sound Archival Recordings, http://sounds.bl.uk

This collection of 44,500 sounds recordings is available for use by staff and students in further and higher education institutions under a free licence. The collection contains many different types of materials including classical music, sounds from nature, spoken word and world and traditional music. Recordings can be downloaded in MP3 format and used in education.

Internet Archive, www.archive.org/index.php

This wide-ranging archive of all sorts of online resources has specific sections for moving images and audio. There is an enormous range of different types of content, including news, feature films and documentaries. Most content is in the public domain and therefore freely available for use in teaching.

Royalty Free Music, www.royaltyfreemusic.com/free.html

This site contains a selection of stock music that is free for download and use in education. Royalty Free is not the same as copyright free. In addition to music the site also contains royalty free stock footage, royalty free sound effects, royalty free clip art, royalty free images and royalty free photos.

Partners in Rhyme, www.partnersinrhyme.com

This site contains royalty free music and sound effects, some for free and others at a very low cost. The site is aimed at amateur and professional multimedia producers, film makers, musicians and students. It provides music, sound effects and audio tools. A selection of music loops and sound effects are available for free download provided that they are not used for commercial purposes.

Conclusion

Multimedia and images are rich sources of content that many teachers want to use in e-learning. However, it is all too easy to fall foul of copyright laws when embedding this type of content into an online course. Advice for teachers is needed early on in the course design process to help them identify copyright-free sources, and to ensure that if permission is required, it is sought in good time. Teachers also need to be educated about licences such as Creative Commons that can help them find good sources of multimedia content. Further sources of advice for training and support specifically related to using multimedia content are listed at the end of the book.

References

EDUCAUSE (2008) *7 Things You Should Know About Lecture Capture*, http://net.educause.edu/ir/library/pdf/ELI7044.pdf [accessed 10 January 2010].

JISC (2006) *Intellectual Property Rights (IPR) in Networked E-Learning*, www.jisclegal.ac.uk/ManageContent/ViewDetail/tabid/243/ID/130/In tellectual-Property-Rights-IPR-in-Networked-E-Learning— 28042006.aspx [accessed 10 January 2010].

Prensky, M. (2001) Digital Natives, Digital Immigrants, *On the Horizon*, NCB University Press, 9 (5), www.marcprensky.com/writing/Prensky%20- %20Digital%20Natives,%20Digital%20Immigrants%20-%20Part1.pdf [accessed 10 Jan 2010].

Secker, J. (2004) *Electronic Resources in the Virtual Learning Environment: a guide for librarians*, Chandos Publishing.

4 Copyright issues and 'born' digital resources

Introduction

This chapter is concerned with what is sometimes called 'born digital' or existing digital content. The term refers to content that is first created in digital format, including word-processed documents, web pages or content that is available through a variety of online databases. This contrasts with material that is digitized from a print or analogue format for either preservation or access reasons. The copyright issues associated with born digital content differ from those associated with digitized material. There is also a large amount of content that already exists in digital format that teachers wish to make use of in e-learning. It is often technically straightforward to incorporate the material into a virtual learning environment. However, the ease with which digital content can be copied and reused is not mirrored by the copyright implications of doing so. The chapter also discusses the copyright and IPR issues associated with teachers' own resources, for example their own teaching materials that are created specifically for use in e-learning, sometimes known as 'learning objects'. The case study in this chapter is from the University of Auckland, who provide an Electronic Course Materials (ECM) service to allow lecturers to include both digitized content and born digital material in their online course.

How is born digital content different?

Born digital content, whether it is a word document, a PDF or an MP3 audio file can easily be downloaded and copied. Distribution of the content is also relatively straightforward if the file is placed on a network or sent via e-mail to multiple recipients. Digital copies are exact copies of the original file, so unlike a scan or a photocopy there is no degradation of quality when digital files are copied. For these reasons and others, those who produce digital content for commercial purposes are often keen to ensure that they retain control over their material. Consequently copyright issues are highly important. Where content is sold commercially via the internet (such as via a subscription database or website), the use or reuse of that content is usually governed by a licence agreement or terms and conditions, therefore contract law rather than copyright law usually applies. Some contracts can limit the rights provided by the copyright laws of a country, so the small print should be consulted carefully before institutional licences for digital resources are signed. In Chapter 1 we saw how in Ireland the copyright act has been amended to ensure that rights such as fair dealing cannot be limited by the licences of electronic resources. However, elsewhere in the world this is not the case, and it is not currently the case in the UK.

Some digital content may be free at the point of use via the internet, but much publisher content is protected due to its commercial value and the significant financial investment associated with its production. There are several ways that copyright can be protected in a digital environment; through licence agreements and through technological measures. Many companies who make digital content available will use a combination of both of these techniques in order to protect their content from misuse. This chapter will first examine digital rights management technologies, which are a technical solution to preventing copyright infringement. It will then explore the terms and conditions and licences associated with several different types of digital resources and how they govern what a teacher or academic can do with the content. Several examples are included to show how website content is protected by commercial and not-for-profit organizations. A number of other examples are included from subscription databases that academic institutions frequently purchase, to illustrate the ways that these commercial companies protect their copyright but might allow it to be reused in an educational context.

Digital rights management

Digital rights management (DRM) is a technological solution to safeguarding rights in the digital environment. Various methods have been developed which can prevent a user from copying material in digital format, for example using encryption techniques or preventing material being printed or downloaded. For those requiring further details, DRM systems are discussed in Pedley (2007, 49–65). However, significantly for readers of this book is the recognition in copyright law that DRM technologies must be respected and that anyone who tries to disable or 'circumvent' such a system can be charged with copyright infringement. In the USA the Digital Millennium Copyright Act (1998) was hugely controversial because of the provision that made it illegal to 'circumvent any DRM technologies'. However, more recently European copyright legislation was also amended to make illegal any attempts to tamper or remove DRM technologies. There are similar attempts underway in Canada, which, as we saw in Chapter 1, have been met with opposition from the education community.

There is a concern that under UK copyright legislation, electronic content is particularly difficult to reuse for educational purposes. Many publishers have taken to defining their services such as e-books as a database, so giving the material both database and copyright protection. The use of the material in these collections is then governed by licences or contracts and by putting DRM protection mechanisms in place, it means that taking advantage of fair dealing can be extremely difficult when reusing born digital resources.

DRM technology impacts on the education community as it is being used by many e-book suppliers to protect their content from being copied. For example, the company Ingram Digital provide e-books through the MyiLibrary platform which is used by academic, medical, professional and public libraries. This platform is popular with libraries as individual titles from a collection almost 100,000 books can be purchased. Other e-books suppliers often sell titles in bundled deals. However, MyiLibrary has DRM in place that restricts how teachers and students can use the content, so for example, only a maximum of ten pages can be printed or downloaded from an e-book. This platform allows tutors to add direct links to chapters from books, or to entire books; however the material must remain on the MyiLibrary platform and cannot be placed into the VLE. The licence is discussed in more detail later in this chapter (see page 114)

JISC have provided a useful tool to allow libraries to compare e-book platforms (www.jisc-adat.com/adat/adat_ebooks.pl) and, of the seven platforms they compare, only Credo Reference does not use DRM. DRM technologies are also common in the music and film industries to protect material and to try to prevent illegal copying. However, in educational settings DRM can restrict the way in which teachers are able to use content, and activities that may be permitted using print-based resources can become complex and potentially illegal. The general advice is not to tamper with any DRM mechanism that is restricting how you can copy or use a work without permission or legal advice, even if you believe you should be able to do this under a copyright exception.

Using content from websites

There is a huge amount of educational material available on the web and this overarching category of resources includes not only text-based websites, but also digital images and multimedia collections (these are discussed in more detail in Chapter 3). When content was first made available on the web many organizations did not consider copyright issues. Few early websites had copyright statements that made it clear to those accessing the information what they were permitted to do with the content. For a number of years many people who were accessing information on the web had misconceptions about what they were able to do with that material. Many people equated 'free to view' as 'free to copy' and while levels of awareness about copyright issues and web-based content is high in the education community compared to elsewhere, misconceptions still remain. In 2009 most large organizations do now include a clear copyright statement on their website and provide further information, for example in terms and conditions, about what can be done with their content. Nevertheless, it seems that relatively few people look at these statements or understand what they might mean.

In general, if you wish to use content from the web in your online course it is usually better to include a link to this material. This largely avoids any copyright issues as the content remains on the website and you are simply directing students to the page where it is hosted. Some teachers claim that linking to the web can be problematic as links might change and this can result in a broken link from their course. While it is true that some organizations do reorganize their websites fairly regularly, usually a check every six months to see if a link is in place should be sufficient. Teachers can also encourage students to report any broken links to them so that they can be repaired quickly. If a teacher adds many links to the web from an online course it can be time-consuming to check that these are still working, but link-checking software can be used to save time. It may also be more appropriate to use some form of bookmarking software, for example delicious social bookmarking (http://delicious.com), which is discussed in Chapter 5. Social bookmarking allows users to manage large numbers of web links, rather than adding these to a reading list or a web page in the VLE.

There can be instances when students are required to access web-based content and a link is insufficient. For example, a course on web design might wish to show several websites and perhaps compare how they looked at different periods in time. In other instances a teacher might have genuine concerns that the content on the site will be removed before the course finishes and so downloading the material is preferable to linking. To assist with advising teachers about using content from the web, this next section includes some examples of websites that make a specific provision for educational use of their site. It also provides some good practice guidelines for teachers who wish to download content from the web and mount it on an e-learning platform.

Website terms and conditions

It is always wise to check the terms and conditions or the copyright statement on a website before using the content in teaching. It is common practice for website terms and conditions to state that the organization assumes you have read and understood their terms and conditions and that in accessing their website you have agreed to be bound by the terms. This is called an 'implicit' licence and in a court of law you might find it difficult to maintain you were not aware of these terms as a link to them will usually be prominent. In fact, almost all websites where you need to register or create some form of personal account, force the user to actively agree to their terms and conditions, usually by checking a box. Commercial websites (such as Amazon, eBay and iTunes) where you are purchasing either a product or a service will also compel users to agree to their terms and conditions before allowing you to place an order. It is common for copyright statements to be included here and if you wish to use content from a commercial site for educational purposes you are well advised to check the statement in some detail. It will be rare for a commercial website to include exceptions for educational use of the site as their primary purpose is a commercial one. Most companies are anxious to safeguard their copyright and will want to protect the use of their content and logo by others.

Example of a commercial website terms and conditions: Amazon

Amazon is a website that many members of the general public will be familiar with, using the site to purchase products such as books, DVDs and CDs. However, Amazon also has many uses in education; for example teachers may wish to highlight to students the books they want them to buy, or to search inside a book to ascertain its relevance to a course. Thus it is not uncommon for teachers to ask about using Amazon content for educational purposes. Lecturers have been known to build online reading lists for their students with accompanying images of book jackets to make the lists more visually attractive. If we examine the Amazon.co.uk website terms and conditions in more detail (Amazon, 2009) we find in the first instance that Amazon state: 'Please read these conditions carefully before using the Amazon.co.uk website. By using the Amazon.co.uk website, you signify your agreement to be bound by these conditions' (Amazon, 2009).

The specific parts of the licence that relate to copyright include:

- Amazon.co.uk grants you a limited licence to access and make personal use of the website, but you are not permitted to download (other than page caching) or modify it, or any portion of it, except with express written consent of Amazon.co.uk.
- You may not frame or use framing techniques to enclose any trademark, logo, or other proprietary information (including images, text, page layout, or form) of Amazon.co.uk and its affiliates without express written consent.
- You are granted a limited, revocable, and non-exclusive right to create a hyperlink to the Welcome page of Amazon.co.uk as long as the link does not portray Amazon.co.uk, its affiliates, or their

products or services in a false, misleading, derogatory, or otherwise offensive matter.

- You may not use any Amazon.co.uk logo or other proprietary graphic or trademark as part of the link without our express written consent.

Therefore, as a teacher it would be sensible to link to the Amazon home page, rather than to use a deep or frame link. Teachers should also not take images or any other content from the site, for example book jacket images, for use in an online reading list. The ownership of the copyright of the content on this site is extremely clear; it states:

- All content included on the website, such as text, graphics, logos, button icons, images, audio clips, digital downloads, data compilations, and software, is the property of Amazon.co.uk, its affiliates or its content suppliers and is protected by Luxembourg and international copyright, authors' rights and database right laws.

(Amazon, 2009)

Anyone wishing to use Amazon content for educational purposes would be advised to contact the company before proceeding.

Non-commercial/not-for-profit websites

In contrast to the above example, non commercial websites often may have more liberal terms and conditions if you wish to use their content for educational purposes. You should still check the terms and conditions of a specific site carefully but may find that educational use is permitted. The authors of the content on these types of sites may be well aware that the education community wishes to use their content.

Non-commercial or not-for-profit websites include the following:

- government or inter-government organizations
  - government department websites
  - other public bodies, for example, the British Library and other national libraries, National Archives

◆ international organizations such as the United Nations, the
World Bank and UNESCO
◆ other educational institutions, for example, schools, universities and
colleges
◆ educational funding bodies, such as JISC and HEFCE
◆ charity websites
◆ websites of special interest groups or professional bodies, for
example, the American Library Association.

Several examples are now provided to illustrate how the terms and
conditions of use of content from these non-commercial organizations
might vary.

Example Terms of Use from UK Department of Communities and Local Government

The Department of Communities and Local Government (DCLG) is a UK
central government department and their website (see Figure 4.1) includes
a copyright statement which is part of the more general terms and
conditions of use. It can be consulted at: www.communities.gov.uk/
corporate/help/conditions.

As with all central government department websites in the UK the
content is subject to Crown Copyright. Crown Copyright material in the
UK is subject to a waiver that means that while it is afforded protection for
125 years the content can be freely reproduced. The site says:

> The Crown copyright protected material (other than departmental or
> agency logos) may be reproduced free of charge in any format or
> medium for research, private study or for internal circulation within
> an organization. This is subject to the material being reproduced
> accurately and not used in a misleading context.
>
> (DCLG, 2010)

This means that a teacher wishing to use this content in the classroom, or
to reproduce the material in the online learning environment, would be
able to do this without needing to request permission and without
payment of a fee. This may be useful as government department websites

Figure 4.1 *DCLG website (8 January 2010), www.communities.gov.uk/corporate*

tend to change fairly regularly and reports can be notoriously difficult to find. In general it would still be advisable to link to content on this website rather than to download the material and host it on an institutional server, but the terms and conditions do allow the latter if required. DCLG clearly state that their logos are not to be reproduced without permission. The reuse of images and logos from websites is often subject to a different set of terms and conditions, largely in order for organizations to protect themselves from misrepresentation or perceived endorsement of other companies that could be potentially damaging.

In this example the terms and conditions of the UNESCO website (see Figure 4.2) reveal that the UN agency devoted to Education, Social and Natural Science, Culture and Communication take a less permissive attitude towards copyright. Their copyright statement is located at the bottom right of the screen and, as is typical with many websites, the terms and conditions apply to anyone who accesses their website. The terms state: 'All contents on this website are protected by copyright. UNESCO is pleased to allow those who may choose to

Figure 4.2 *UNESCO website, http://portal.unesco.org*

access the site to download and copy the materials for their personal, non-commercial use.'

If a teacher wishes to use content from this site they would be advised to provide a link to this material rather than download it. Educational use is not explicitly mentioned and 'personal, non-commercial' may not extend to hosting the material on a virtual learning environment.

The UNESCO site goes on to state:

Any copy made of the materials must retain all copyright and other proprietary legends and notices in the same form and manner as on the original. Any use of textual and multimedia information (sound, image, software, etc.) in the website shall be accompanied by an acknowledgement of the source, citing the uniform resource locator (URL) of the page (Title of the material, © UNESCO, URL).

No other use of the materials is authorised without prior written permission from UNESCO.

Further details are also provided in a terms of use statement, which includes information about hyperlinking to the UNESCO site and getting permission. Users are advised to link to the top level of the site, rather than to engage in deep linking as UNESCO cannot guarantee that deep links will persist. Again the logos are protected and must not be used without express permission.

Good practice guidelines

The following good practice guidelines should be helpful for anyone wishing to use website content in e-learning:

◆ Where possible link to content on the web rather than downloading it and ensure links open in a new browser window.

◆ Do not use frame links which mean that content opens within an e-learning system as it may be unclear that the content is coming from an external source.

◆ Check the website terms and conditions to see if deep links to a site are permitted – if they are, be aware that these may change if the website is reorganized.

◆ If deep links are not permitted, links should go to the home page of an organization and students can be given navigational information to locate the specific part of the website you wish them to consult.

◆ If you feel it is essential to download material, check the terms and conditions or copyright notice on the site before you copy the material.

◆ If you include a screen-shot of a website, include details of the date that the screen-shot was made.

◆ If you are unsure if the site can be downloaded for educational use, check for any contact details and ask permission before downloading the material.

◆   Retain any permissions received for website reuse in an appropriate rights management system so that any subsequent teachers are clear that permission was obtained.

Content from publishers

There is an increasing range of scholarly resources available from publishers in digital format including electronic journals, electronic books and other subscription databases. These resources also include material such as law reports, conference papers or other full text documents. This section will examine e-journals and e-books in some detail before considering a selection of subscription databases, all of which are governed by licences. In the UK, the JISC has made considerable efforts through JISC Collections to negotiate more favourable licences for the further and higher education sectors. The JISC Model Licences (JISC, n.d.) and the NESLI (National Electronic Site Licence Initiative) are intended to help students and staff make effective use of electronic resources in teaching, learning and research. They are also attempts to provide a consistent approach to the access and use of online resources so allowing users to exploit the content to its fullest potential in support of their activities. Examples of some of the activities that the model licences permit include:

◆   searching the online resource and looking at the results on-screen
◆   saving parts electronically; these can be saved to a computer hard drive, floppy disk, CD-ROM, USB flash drive, and so forth
◆   printing out single copies of parts of the online resource, for example, journal articles, images, book chapters, search results, and so on.

More importantly for e-learning they also permit:

◆   Staff and students 'incorporating' parts of the online resource in teaching materials and coursework providing it is appropriately acknowledged. This provides the flexibility to use such items as learning objects.

◆ Staff cutting and pasting extracts from the online resources in printed or electronic course packs for teaching students of the institution. This is not limited to a particular medium and can include teaching materials on CD or through authenticated access to institutional VLEs or intranet. Teaching staff may use extracts to create interactive tutorials that use still and moving images, text and graphics. Staff may also reproduce extracts in a format that aids accessibility, for example, Braille.

The terms of the JISC Model Licences are broad and cover much of the copying that staff might wish to undertaken in e-learning. However, unfortunately these licences are a starting point for negotiations with publishers. Many publisher agreements are modified to remove the more permissive activities specified in the model agreement. Therefore, institutional licences must be studied in detail before copying is undertaken.

Journals

It is now common for academic journals to be published in electronic format, and while many print journals still exist, in the last ten years the higher education community – including lecturers, librarians and students – has embraced journal content in electronic format. In general teachers and academic staff have little need to purchase personal subscriptions to journal content but rely instead on an institutional subscription. Journal subscriptions are usually purchased by the institutional library and a typical site licence will allow staff and students to access the content. With improvements in authentication systems, access to titles is often possible from off-campus as well, using passwords such as Athens or Shibboleth or through a proxy server. Journal licensing has become a complex area for academic libraries, with some titles sold in bundles from aggregators, such as EBSCO, Ingenta or Swetswise. Smaller journal publishers such as scholarly societies tend to use an aggregator service to host their content. Meanwhile large journal publishers such as Oxford University Press have a dedicated platform to host their e-journal content. This means that when purchasing journal titles there is a variety of purchasing options and models. For example, some print journal subscriptions have complementary access to the electronic version while other electronic journals are licensed in bundled deals, which may lead to institutions subscribing to titles in electronic format that may fall outside the scope of their traditional collection policy. This complex landscape means that licences that regulate what a teacher can do with the content from an e-journal can vary tremendously.

In the UK, the JISC attempted to provide some form of consistency for those in higher and further education, by developing model licences and encouraging aggregators and journal publishers to use these. However, invariably different institutions negotiate different agreements with publishers to meet their specific requirements and to try to get the best price. Consequently understanding how electronic journal content can be reused in e-learning is a complicated business for library staff and many teachers and academic staff are left baffled. Where an institution has multiple subscriptions to large numbers of journals it makes sense for the licence agreements to be managed by library staff. Library staff often have the best understanding of what can be done with e-journal content and may need to advise teachers. For example, many journals do not permit PDF articles to be downloaded from their site and mounted within the virtual learning environment. Yet, many teachers fail to see how this practice differs from providing students with a deep link to the article on the publisher's website. In fact, by downloading an article it will mean that journal publishers are unable to accurately record journal usage. It also means that the PDF is available to students even if an institution cancels their subscription. For this reason it is usually advisable to encourage teaching staff to link to journal content. Many publishers are now using Digital Object Identifiers (DOIs) as a stable or persistent way of maintaining a link to journal articles. This process has got far easier in recent years, but is still complex.

Digital Object Identifiers, www.doi.org

Many e-journals are hosted on databases and creating stable links to material within these systems used to be difficult. Digital Object Identifiers are a standard way of identifying and managing digital content and a useful way of creating a stable link to content from e-journals. DOIs are a unique reference for identifying a piece of digital content, independent of the publisher or platform that might hold it. The system is managed by the International DOI Foundation, which is an open membership consortium and includes both commercial and non-commercial partners. It is not restricted to e-journals, but all types of digital content. Once a DOI number is registered, it can be used to create a stable link to the item by using a link resolver.

E-journal licence agreements

Two examples of e-journal licences are examined below to highlight some of the approaches to licensing digital content. The specific clauses that cover how the material can be used in e-learning are discussed.

Project Muse, www.jisc-adat.com/adat/adat_ebooks.pl

Project Muse represents a collaboration between libraries and publishers and provides full-text access to a selection of around 400 humanities and social sciences journals. Access to titles is comparatively inexpensive and titles are available from many of the world's leading university presses and scholarly societies. The journal has a reasonably permissive approach to how its content can be used in a subscribing institution. An example of the standard subscription licence is available from the Project Muse website (Project Muse, 2009). However, the following is an example from the general licence and subscribing institutions will need to consult the agreement they sign:

The licence includes a section of permitted acts that include allowing users to:

◆ distribute a copy of individual articles of items of the licensed materials in print or electronic form to Authorized Users, including the distribution of a copy for non-commercial educational purposes to each individual student (Authorized User) in a class at a Subscriber's institution
◆ use a persistent URL, or durable URL, to the licensed materials, including full-text articles, for courses of instruction offered by the Subscribing Institution, where access is restricted to students enrolled on the course, to instructors, and to library staff maintaining

the link, and such access is limited to the duration of the course. Each item should carry an appropriate acknowledgment of the source, copyright, and publisher, and the links to such items shall be deleted by the Subscriber when they are no longer required for such a purpose.

JSTOR licence, www.jstor.org

JSTOR is a not-for-profit organization that was founded in 1995 by the Andrew W. Mellon foundation as a solution to the storage problems academic libraries were facing managing journal collections. Particularly in the arts and humanities, scholars often require access to historical journal material. JSTOR has been a tremendous success story and extremely popular with both researchers and students. In 2009 JSTOR merged with a company called Ithaka (www.ithaka.org), another not-for-profit organization. The JSTOR collection focuses on preserving digitized back runs of journals covering the humanities, social sciences and sciences. In many instances the most up-to-date issues of a journal are hosted directly by a publisher or by an aggregator, but JSTOR have concentrated their efforts in digitizing historical material and ensuring complete back runs of scholarly publications are available to subscribing institutions.

The following information comes from the general licence available on the JSTOR website and subscribers will need to consult their institutional licence. However it covers licensees and authorizes users to: 'search, view, reproduce, display, download, print, perform, and distribute Content in the JSTOR Archive provided they abide by the restrictions in Sections 2.2 and elsewhere in these Terms and Conditions of Use, for the following Permitted Uses' (JSTOR, 2009a).

'Permitted Uses' are then defined as the following types of activities: research activities; classroom or organizational instruction; student assignments; as part of a scholarly, cultural, educational or organizational presentation or workshop; in research papers or dissertations (with some caveats); and by linking. In addition, the licence is generous to include sharing small amounts of the text with others for non-commercial gain and 'for purposes of collaboration, comment, or the scholarly exchange of ideas'. It also specifically mentions fair use and the educational exceptions of other copyright laws.

Linking to content hosted by JSTOR is often the most efficient way of using this content in e-learning. All JSTOR journals have title and article level stable links, (known here as Stable Universal Resource Locators [URLs]) clearly marked in their database. This means that teachers can use these links to provide direct access to reading materials. There is detailed information on the JSTOR website (JSTOR, 2009b) about how to create stable links to journal articles or titles. However, JSTOR do not use Digital Object Identifiers that have been adopted as a standard open-URL linking procedure by much of the publishing industry.

Case Study 5: The Electronic Course Material service of the University of Auckland Library, New Zealand

Upeksha Amarathunga and Ursula Loots

Introduction

This chapter presents a case study of the Electronic Course Material service of the University of Auckland Library. The University of Auckland was established in 1883 and is New Zealand's leading, and largest, university. The University is spread over five campuses with 38,500 students studying across eight faculties (University of Auckland, 2009).

The University of Auckland Library system includes the General Library, 12 specialist libraries and four Information Commons facilities. The Library is the most extensive library system in New Zealand and is a national leader in providing and developing electronic resources. The Library ranks with the top five Australian university libraries (The University of Auckland Library, 2009a).

The Electronic Course Material service

The ECM service was developed in 2003 after the New Zealand universities renegotiated the agreement with the Copyright Licensing Limited. CLL is New Zealand's copyright clearance centre.

The ECM service makes prescribed and recommended journal articles, book chapters, book extracts, conference papers, case law and parliamentary materials available online for student coursework in all subject areas. The service is managed by the Short Loan department in the Kate Edger Information Commons on the City Campus. Short Loan provides a centralized service for the submission, processing, production and copyright management of readings for all subject areas (The University of Auckland Library, 2009b). Decentralized processing takes place in the Sylvia Ashton-Warner Library on the Epsom (Faculty of Education) campus and in the Philson Library on the Grafton (Faculty of Medicine) campus. In July 2009 there were 9273 items in the collection.

The process

Academic staff members, course co-ordinators and subject librarians submit requests for an electronic copy to be made via an online form on the Library web page (www.library.auckland.ac.nz). The requester's details are automatically populated in the request form. All the requests are captured into a locally developed Course Material Request Administration Database (CoMRAD). CoMRAD provides a localized requesting and administrative platform for the requester and the ECM service staff. The application records and tracks details of requests and associated workflows for electronic and print materials submitted via the online request form.

There are two basic types of electronic course materials (see Amarathunga, 2009, 5):

1   Original material in print only format, such as chapters or extracts from books, journal articles or conference proceedings. If the item is available in the Library, it is digitized and stored in a local e-reserves repository. If an item not held locally, the Library will endeavour to purchase it and if it is out of print, obtain it via interloan.
2   Born digital material such as full-text database articles, web pages and conference reports that can be accessed online. Metadata and a stable link is created enabling students to access the material in the publisher's database.

Copyright compliance

Requests are checked for copyright compliance using the guidelines set out in the CLL licence with New Zealand universities. The guidelines allow for multiple photocopying of extracts from books, periodicals and journals for educational purposes as follows (Copyright Licensing Limited, 2009):

◆   up to 10% or one chapter of a work, whichever is greater
◆   up to 15 pages of all or part of a single work in a collection of works even if the work is published separately, for example, a published compilation of poems, plays or short stories
◆   one or part of one article from a periodical publication, or additional articles from the same periodical publication if they are on the same subject
◆   an artistic work (such as a diagram or illustration) only where copied as part of a textual work
◆   a complete work, only where the work is out of print or unavailable in sufficient quantity within a reasonable time at the normal price (subject to prior written approval from CLL).

The following resources are consulted for requests with complex copyright issues:

◆   use of Copyright Materials 2009, an internal document for the University of Auckland staff, compiled by the University's Copyright Officer
◆   the Copyright Act 1994 and Amendments: Guidelines for Librarians, produced by the Copyright Task Force of the Library and Information Association of New Zealand Aotearoa (LIANZA) (http://lianza.org.nz/library/files/store_022/LIANZA_Copyright_Guidelines_March_2009.pdf).

It is the responsibility of the requester to obtain permission from the copyright holder if they wish to digitize material exceeding the CLL copyright compliance limits. A Copyright Warranty Consent Form (www.library.auckland.ac.nz/slc/copyrightwarrantyconsentform.pdf) has to be completed and sent to the ECM service before material in this category is digitized.

Database licences are checked to ensure that electronic items can be made accessible. A spreadsheet, with the relevant licence information, is maintained by the Library Serials department.

Access

The University of Auckland Library uses the Voyager Library Management System. The digitized items are linked to Course Reserves Lists in the Reserves module within Voyager. Students, academic staff members and subject librarians can access these through the Voyager Course Materials Search tab (www.library.auckland.ac.nz). Course materials are searchable by course number and displayed alphabetically by title. Only members of the University of Auckland can access the digitized material using the University's authentication system to prevent external users from gaining access to copyright-controlled items in the collection (Amarathunga, 2009, 8).

Copyright statement

The CLL compliance guidelines require that a Copyright Warning Notice accompanies every electronic course material item. The following copyright statement is on the Course Materials Search page (http://voyager.auckland. ac.nz/cgi-bin/Pwebrecon.cgi?DB=local&PAGE=rbSearch):

> Course Materials are protected by copyright and are provided solely for the educational purposes of the University. Some works are provided under licence. You may not sell, alter or further reproduce or distribute any course material to any other person. You may only print from it for your own private study and research. Failure to comply with the terms of this warning may expose you to legal action for copyright infringement and/or disciplinary action by the University.

Advantages of the ECM service

Electronic course material has several advantages (Amarathunga, 2009, 19; Holley, 2005, 1):

◆ Improved access
  ◆ 24/7 availability
  ◆ no geographical barriers
  ◆ multiple users able to access the same item simultaneously
  ◆ no danger of theft and mutilation as was the situation with the print collection.

◆ Enhanced service delivery
  ◆ students can print or download articles resulting in longer access
  ◆ students and lecturers save time accessing items.
◆ Improved management of collections
  ◆ avoiding duplication of items when required for more than one course
  ◆ saving staff time on the circulation of physical materials
  ◆ lecturers are able to see remotely the full-text of items placed on short loan, making it easier for them to request additions and removal of items
  ◆ lecturers know when their requests have been processed and are available
◆ Expansion of the range of library resources that are electronically accessible, thereby increasing the availability of resources for:
  ◆ flexible learning courses
  ◆ remote students, who may be unable to get to the library during opening hours.
◆ Ability to access any number of items in addition to the library's borrowing limit for print material.

Issues

There has been a significant increase in the demand for the service over the years; see Table 4.1.

However, research done by Amarathunga (2009) showed a high variation in

Table 4.1 *Increase in items available, digitized and accessed over years*

Academic year	Course materials available		New material added		Usage (page views)	
	Total number	% increase	Total number	% increase	Total number	% increase
2005	5309		1582		266,846	
2006	5700	7.4	1939	22.6	362,175	35.7
2007	6979	22.4	2550	31.5	826,094	128.1*
2008	9273	32.9	2967	16.4	900,669	9.0

*There was a significant increase in the Faculty of Education staff adoption of the ECM service in 2007, contributing to the substantial percentage increase in usage.

the demand for the ECM service in different subject disciplines. According to Amarathunga (2009, 69) the ECM service does not get promoted uniformly throughout all the academic departments of the University of Auckland. The research also revealed that the uptake and usage of the ECM service by academic staff members often depends on the academic staff awareness of the ECM service.

Conclusion

The exponential expansion of the service since its initiation bears witness to the success of the service. The ECM service has improved availability and access to course materials, management of collections and enhanced service delivery. It is recommended that further investigation is done to identify barriers to the use of the service by academics and ways to promote its advantages and usage (Amarathunga, 2009, 75).

References

Amarathunga, U. S. (2009) *Factors Affecting Staff Demand for an Electronic Course Materials Service*, unpublished Masters Dissertation, Victoria University of Wellington.

Copyright Licensing Limited (2009) *Educational*. Retrieved 17 June 2009, from the Copyright Licensing website, www.copyright.co.nz/Educational/ [accessed 10 January 2010].

Holley, R. (2005). *The E-Reserve Project at the University of Auckland: electronic provision of short loan/desk copy articles 2003–2004*. Retrieved 17 June 2009, from The University of Auckland Library website, www.library.auckland.ac.nz/docs/digital_projects/ereserve.pdf [accessed 10 January 2010].

The University of Auckland Library (2009a) *The University of Auckland Facts and Figures* (Jan 2009). Retrieved 16 June 2009, from The University of Auckland Library website, www.library.auckland.ac.nz/about/library_facts_figures.pdf [accessed 10 January 2010].

The University of Auckland Library (2009b) *The Electronic Course Materials Service*. Retrieved 16 June 2009, from The University of Auckland Library website, www.library.auckland.ac.nz/slc/ECMservice.htm [accessed 10 January 2010].

University of Auckland (2009) *2009–2010 The University of Auckland Profile.* Retrieved 1 July 2009, from the University of Auckland website, www.auckland.ac.nz/webdav/site/central/shared/about/the-university/at-a-glance/documents/profile2009-2010.pdf [accessed 10 January 2010].

E-books

E-books are a growing market in the higher and further education community. E-book licensing is more complex than journals as the publishing community have been concerned about the impact that digital access might have on book sales. Whereas academic journals tended to be bought by libraries in the past, book sales in the UK are estimated to be worth £5 million to the economy. In education, text book sales are also incredibly commercially valuable. When e-books first were launched in the late 1990s publishers tried out different models of licensing this content. For example Net Library, launched in 1998, first started offering e-books for sale using a model that allowed for each title to be accessed by only one user at any one time. If a library wanted to allow multiple access then additional 'copies' of the e-book needed to be purchased. From the perspective of teachers and students the concept of e-books clearly implies that access to titles should not be limited to one user, so many e-book publishers have now recognized that the this model is not desirable. E-books were also slow to take off because of the restrictive way that titles were sold in bundles, rather than individually. This meant that until relatively recently few libraries found that not enough books in bundled collections were on lecturers' reading lists. MyiLibrary changed this model by allowing individual titles to be purchased. However, even in 2009 JISC was still aware that the value and future of e-books was unclear. This led JISC Collections to negotiate free access to 36 titles from MyiLibrary for all higher education institutions (until August 2009) as part of the National E-book Observatory Consultation (JISC, 2007). This project has been gathering evidence from librarians, students and academic staff to inform the future development of licensing of e-books. Further trials are still on-going, but given the substantial investment from JISC in e-learning, ensuring that e-books can be used to support current teaching methods will be crucial.

Meanwhile, at the present time, as is the case with many electronic resources, what a tutor can do with content from an e-book is largely governed by the licence agreement rather than by copyright laws. Many e-books also tend to be available in proprietary formats, which discourage or prevent users from downloading or printing significant portions of the content.

MyiLibrary, www.myilibrary.com

MyiLibrary is a subscription e-book service provided by Ingram Digital that numerous academic and public libraries are now using to enhance their collections. Like most e-book platforms the company use DRM technologies to restrict copying and downloading from their site. However, the e-books are popular because they do not require users to install any specific reader software. Most titles are in PDF format, so can be read in the free Adobe Acrobat Reader. They can also be read by multiple users and be purchased on a title-by-title basis. The Terms and Conditions for the use of their content is available on their website (Ingram Digital, 2009). Content can only be downloaded for personal, non-commercial use, and the download limits are set at ten pages per book. This means that if a tutor wanted to use this content in e-learning they would need to include a link to the material.

Google Books, http://books.google.co.uk

While not strictly an e-book platform, at this point it is worth considering Google Books (http://books.google.co.uk) which is an ambitious digitization project representing a joint venture between Google and several large academic libraries including Harvard, MIT, Yale and Oxford. Launched in 2004, Google Books has been stalled by many copyright issues, which have given rise to a large scale and widely publicized legal challenge by publishers in the United States. In 2006 an action was brought against Google by the Association of American Publishers and the Authors

Guild for copyright infringement. For the past three years this has meant access to titles via Google Books has been somewhat erratic. As the case progressed, Google made frequent modifications to the service, meaning that Google Books rarely looked or behaved the same from week to week. At one point users were required to set up a Google account in order to get access to any full text. More recently, limited previews have been available from certain publishers, snippets of text for others and full text available only for some out of copyright material. The constantly changing nature of the service has meant that few teachers would consider relying on content provided through Google Books.

However, the Google Book settlement agreement reached in the United States District Court for the Southern District of New York in November 2008 may change this. The agreement was stalled in October 2009, but promises to address publishers' concerns about the project through establishing a system of payments to rights holders and an independent registry to regulate the usage of 'orphan works'. The hearing was adjourned on the grounds that the court needed to approve the final document and it was still undergoing changes. A revised agreement was issued in November 2009, and while UK and US publishers are included, the rest of the European Union has been dropped from the agreement. While Google Books does not provide an e-book platform, it does offer enormous potential as a means of providing access to out-of-copyright book material. If a settlement can be reached it will give educational institutions a greater degree of confidence about linking to material on this platform. However, at the time of going to press, Google Books had faced another legal challenge, this time from French publishers, again citing copyright infringement. This case is an example of where scanning material under the fair use provision in US is not permitted under the laws of other countries. Recent news reports (BBC, 2009) also demonstrated how European countries are split over the issues. It is too early to speculate on the impact Google Books might have on other e-book platforms; however, if access to titles can be maintained and procedures for stable linking can be established, this service offers much to the e-learning community in terms of full text content. Further information about the settlement, including the full text of the agreement, is available from the Google Books site: http://books.google.com/googlebooks/agreement/press.html.

Databases and other subscription resources

The distinction between electronic journals, e-books and databases is often extremely tenuous. In fact many e-book and e-journal providers define their product as a database to award it extra protection under intellectual property laws. Using content from databases will always be governed by licence agreements; however some countries have ensured that educational exceptions in their law cannot be overwritten. Educational licences are available for a variety of commercial databases used in professions such as law and business. For example, legal databases such as Westlaw (www.westlaw.co.uk) and Lawtel (www.lawtel.com) offer educational licences. The legal and news database Lexis-Nexis (www.lexisnexis.com) also offer special licences for educational establishments. Similarly, business schools might well subscribe to databases such as Thomson Reuters DataStream (www.datastream.com), Bloomberg (www.bloomberg.com) or one of the databases provided by Wharton Research Data Services (http://wrds.wharton.upenn.edu).

One of the problems with some of the professional databases listed above is that they are notoriously complex to search. Many are not primarily aimed at the education sector so the search interface is unfamiliar to students used to using simple search engines. Lecturers and tutors are often tempted to download this content and provide students with the material in an easy-to-use format in the VLE. However, teachers and lecturers will need to be extremely careful if they wish to extract or copy content from these sources. The two legal databases Westlaw and Lexis have developed tools that allow teachers to create deep links to documents in their database, so removing the need to download content and place it on a network for students. However, because of the commercial nature of these particular databases, downloading content and mounting it on an e-learning platform is rarely permitted.

This next section will briefly examine two licences for databases. The Westlaw education licence is examined as this provides an example of a commercial database that has an educational licence. EBSCO Online Research Databases (www2.ebsco.com) are then examined, as this database holds an enormous variety of electronic content, including indexing and abstracting services such as International Bibliographic of the Social Sciences and PsychInfo, full text electronic journals, e-books and a variety of services for the library community. It also offers licences to the higher education sector, to schools, healthcare organizations, government departments and other companies. Once again, the general licence is used as an example and institutions subscribing to these databases should check their own licence agreement for variations.

Westlaw UK Subscriber Agreement

Westlaw UK have a subscriber agreement available on their website (Thomson Reuters, 2009). This agreement lists a number of 'permitted acts' that authorized users are allowed to undertake. In terms of copying material for use in e-learning, the licence on first sight appears relatively permissive stating that users can: (b) reproduce, quote and excerpt Extracts in Subscriber's own Work Product.

The term 'Work Product' is defined in the agreement as meaning print or electronic course packs, including legal research manuals and learning guides but intranet, extranet or internet sites are specifically excluded unless a separate agreement is made. The agreement also specifically excludes the storage of the material and suggests that this is permitted only on a temporary basis. Therefore, it seems unlikely that downloaded material could be stored within an e-learning system on a regular basis, without a separate agreement to permit this.

Nevertheless, Westlaw UK responded to requests from UK universities to allow stable links to content to be created by tutors. Westlaw Representatives can provide lecturers and e-learning staff with personal accounts to access Westlaw which, in addition to the regular search function, also include a 'build link' option when viewing any piece of content on the database. Clicking on this option gives the tutor a stable link which can be inserted into the e-learning platform to direct students straight to the article. By using this tool users can stay within the terms of the Westlaw Subscriber Agreement but create direct links to full text content from an e-learning platform.

EBSCO Online Research Databases, www2.ebsco.com

The EBSCO licence (EBSCO, 2009a) states that: 'the Licensee and Sites may not reproduce, distribute, display, modify, transfer or transmit, in any form, or by any means, any Database or Service or any portion thereof without the prior written consent of EBSCO, except as specifically authorized in this Agreement'.

The terms go on to specify that: 'the Licensee and Authorized Users may download or print limited copies of citations, abstracts, full text or portions thereof provided the information is used solely in accordance with copyright law. Licensee and Authorized Users may not publish the information'.

Similar to JSTOR, the electronic journal database discussed earlier, EBSCO make provision for users to create stable links to items in their database. This allows lecturers to create online reading lists that link out to content on the EBSCO platform, without requiring the material to be downloaded. They provide advice about setting up database, title and article level links in their Training and Support website (EBSCO, 2009b). The links are called 'persistent links' and mean that content can be easily included in an e-learning course. EBSCO also allow subscribers to download logos, buttons and icons that can be used subject to terms and conditions in library guides, handouts and in e-learning to promote the databases. They also have a Search Box Builder tool, which allows a customized EBSCO search box to be created and used as appropriate in your institution. This search box could also be made available to students through the virtual learning environment.

Lecturers' own digital content: teaching materials

This next section will consider the copyright issues associated with digital content created by lecturers. Many teachers use an e-learning platform to distribute their own teaching materials to students, such as course handbooks, reading lists, lecture notes and PowerPoint presentations. The advantage for students is that they can pick up this material at a time and place convenient to them. Teaching materials for full-time students are often distributed in this manner, in addition to using e-learning for distributing content to distance learning students who don't attend face-to-face teaching. Most of this material is relatively unproblematic in terms of copyright if it has been authored by the lecturer or teacher in question. As an employee, copyright in these materials will usually lie with the institution. Some universities have attempted to formalize the IPR situation with teaching materials, whereas others have not. In their report in 2006,

JISC recommended that all universities in the UK had a clearly stated IPR policy to make it clear where ownership of teaching materials lay. Institutions without such a policy (it is unlikely for example that many schools or colleges will have one) would be wise to develop an IPR policy to clarify this situation. Those who are concerned about restricting academic freedom should take heed of the policies developed by leading universities, which aim to strike a balance between ensuring that staff have the freedom to retain ownership of their teaching materials whilst giving the university the right to use teaching materials in e-learning. A selection of University IPR and copyright policies are included in the Conclusion for those requiring further guidance in this area (see page 192).

More complex copyright issues can arise when content is included in teaching materials from elsewhere. For example, a lecturer may include images in a PowerPoint slide that they have downloaded from the internet, or lecture notes might include excerpts from a published work. Many lecturers are routinely given editing rights for the courses they teach in a VLE, which means that they are responsible for uploading their own teaching materials. This type of 'third-party content' can easily end up being available online, with little consideration of the copyright implications. Moreover, this is a case where, in a traditional classroom, including this material in teaching materials would not require the item to be copied. Or if it was copied then a single copy would usually be made and the teacher could claim they were doing this under fair dealing for criticism and review. E-learning by its very nature means that copies are placed on a network, potentially infringing the copyright. Ensuring that staff are given adequate support and training about copyright issues when creating teaching materials for use in e-learning is therefore vital. Training is discussed in further detail in Chapter 6.

Learning objects

Learning objects are a group of digital assets created and arranged with specific learning objectives in mind. They may be relatively simple technically, such as a series of web pages followed by quiz questions to test understanding, whereas more complex learning objects might also include video or other forms of multimedia. In recent years the e-learning community has invested considerably in creating learning objects that can be re-purposed and reused with new content, so the structure of the object becomes as important as the content. E-learning professionals and teachers have been encouraging the sharing of learning objects through deposit in repositories. For example JISC established a learning object repository called Jorum (www.jorum.ac.uk) in 2006 to facilitate the sharing of learning objects in further and higher education in the UK. Other learning object repositories exist around the world, for example MERLOT (Multimedia Educational Resource for Learning and Online Teaching) (www.merlot.org/merlot/index.htm) in the USA which contains peer-reviewed resources for faculty and students in higher education. Meanwhile LORN is an Australian learning object repository (http://lorn.flexiblelearning.net.au) which contains materials for the vocational sector. In Europe the Learning Resource Exchange (http://lreforschools.eun.org/LRE-Portal/Index.iface) is a repository containing materials for schools from 18 European countries. These repositories are particularly popular with schools where teachers frequently share teaching materials.

Copyright issues are particularly pertinent in the learning object field as sharing and the need to provide open access are often part of the requirement under which content is deposited. Anyone depositing material in a learning object repository must ensure that they own the copyright in the resource or have the appropriate permissions. Meanwhile, anyone wanting to use a learning object from a repository will need to familiarize themselves with the licence agreement and ensure that if they re-purpose the material they follow any specified terms and conditions. The Jorum repository, for example, now uses a Creative Commons License to regulate the use of objects in their collection. This means that those reusing learning objects from Jorum must release their resulting content under the same licence terms.

Student-owned content

Another final area that also needs to be considered is digital content that students might upload to an e-learning platform. E-learning systems are not simply delivery mechanisms for institutional or third content, but students are expected to contribute content sometimes as part of the assessment process. For example, most virtual learning environments have a discussion board or 'online forum' where students submit messages or queries to their tutors. Online submission of assignments such as essays or short pieces of writing is also frequently possible in VLEs, and tools such as wikis and blogs are increasingly being used for collaborative writing in education. Where students are expected to participate in online activities, then teachers, educational developers and e-learning professionals need to consider the copyright implications. Students will own the copyright to all of their work, whether it is a contribution to a discussion board, an essay they submit as part of their coursework or their final dissertation. Therefore, if the tutor wishes to copy or reuse this work, they need to obtain permission from the students. While many universities have modified student regulations to mandate that students use some form of e-learning (for example, for online submission of work) this does not mean that the institution owns the copyright of the students' work. It would be good practice to create a release form that students can complete if the institution wishes to retain and reuse student work, for example to compile a database of frequently asked questions, or to provide subsequent groups with access to example dissertations or essays.

With increasing numbers of PhD theses being submitted in digital format and moves to digitize theses as part of a preservation strategy, copyright can present several problems. Some institutions require that doctoral students assign some of their rights to the institution awarding the degree. However, in many instances copyright is retained by the student as the author of the thesis. In practice this means that lecturers should not distribute a thesis without permission from the author. Libraries meanwhile are only able to grant permission for copying under fair dealing and cannot digitize a print thesis without permission from the student. Theses are also problematic because under the examination exception in UK law, third-party content can be included in the thesis, although permission needs to be sought for any subsequent publication. Consequently, institutions digitizing theses need to obtain permission from the students and then decide how to proceed if third-party content is found. In the case of storing theses for long term use in e-learning, it will usually be more appropriate to use the institutional repository rather than the VLE. By depositing theses in a repository, copyright issues can be resolved and the material can then be placed on open access. Teachers can then add a stable link to the thesis in the repository if they wish to direct other students to the work.

Conclusions and general advice

Contracts and licence agreements tend to take precedent over copyright laws when determining how existing digital content can be used in e-learning. This makes it difficult to generalize about what can and what cannot be done. It is important that teachers and e-learning professionals check the terms of licence agreements in some detail before proceeding. While it should not be the case that contracts are more restrictive than the law, in practice DRM mechanisms can mean that it might be difficult to use the content in e-learning when compared to what might have occurred in the classroom. For example, some e-books restrict the number of pages that can be printed and some e-journal providers will monitor the number of downloads and suspend access to a title if they suspect excessive copying might be undertaken. This chapter has attempted to summarize the different ways that digital content from publishers, website owners, academics and students can be used in e-learning. Further reading is suggested in the Conclusion in addition to the references below.

References

Amazon (2009) *Conditions of Use and Sale*,
www.amazon.co.uk/gp/help/customer/display.html/ref=footer_cou?ie=UTF8&nodeId=1040616 [accessed 10 January 2010].

BBC (2009, 13 November) *Europe Split on Google Book Plans*,
http://news.bbc.co.uk/1/hi/programmes/click_online/8357773.stm [accessed 10 January 2010].

DCLG (2010) Department of Communities and Local Government copyright statement,
www.communities.co.uk/corporate/help/conditions.

EBSCO (2009a) *Terms of Use*,
http://support.ebscohost.com/ehost/terms.html [accessed 10 January 2010].

EBSCO (2009b) *EBSCO Support and Training*,
http://support.ebsco.com [accessed 10 January 2010].

Ingram Digital (2009) *Ingram Digital Terms and Agreement*,
http://ingramdigital.com/legal/terms-and-conditions [accessed 10 January 2010].

JISC (2007) *National E-book Observatory Project*,

www.jiscebooksproject.org [accessed 10 January 2010].

JISC Collections (n.d.) *A Guide to the JISC Model Licences*,
www.jisc-collections.ac.uk/model_licence/coll_guide_jiscmodel. aspx
[accessed 10 January 2010].

JSTOR (2009a) *JSTOR Terms and Conditions of Use*,
www.jstor.org/page/info/about/policies/terms.jsp [accessed 10
January 2010].

JSTOR (2009b) *JSTOR Linking Features*,
www.jstor.org/page/info/resources/librarians/linking.jsp [accessed 10
January 2010].

Pedley, P. (2007) *Digital Copyright*, 2nd edn, Facet Publishing.

Project MUSE (2009) *Project MUSE Institutional Subscriber Licensing
Agreement*,
http://muse.jhu.edu/about/subscriptions/license_review.html
[accessed 10 January 2010].

Thomson Reuters (2009) *Westlaw UK Subscriber Agreement*,
www.westlaw.co.uk/terms_conditions/index.shtm [accessed 12
February 2010].

5 Copyright in the emerging digital environment

Introduction

The internet and associated web-based technologies have developed significantly in the past five years, with new tools to facilitate communication and interactivity. At the same time we have also seen more powerful personal computers and web-enabled mobile devices along with increased availability and a reduction in cost of high-speed broadband networks. The Digital Britain report (DCMS, 2009) highlighted many of these developments and recent Ofcom statistics showed that broadband access in the home in the UK grew from 13% in 2003 to 67% in 2008 (Ofcom, 2009). Increased connectivity has changed the ways in which learning can be delivered to students, meaning any time, anywhere learning is becoming a real possibility. At the same time we have seen a growing range of more sophisticated web-based tools and services, many of which are simple to use and free at the point of use. This chapter focuses on what some have called the new or 'emerging' technologies being used in education and the associated copyright issues. These technologies are sometimes referred to as 'Web 2.0' technologies, including blogs, wikis, social media and social networking sites, but the chapter also briefly considers other developments in e-learning such as mobile learning and cloud computing. The focus here is not on these technologies *per se*, but on any specific copyright issues that arise from their use. Suggested further reading is included in the Conclusion of the book, for example Cornish (2009, 164–6) who examines some of the copyright issues associated with Web 2.0 services.

The chapter starts by focusing on a number of tools and services that are currently being used either by individual teachers or educational institutions, including social networking sites and social media sites. It then considers the copyright issues associated with using third-party hosted materials, including where copyright lies in works created by multiple authors and who owns copyright of content uploaded to Web 2.0 services. The chapter provides examples of how several Web 2.0 services handle copyright in terms of protecting their own rights, as many are commercial websites that are funded largely from advertising revenues. However it also considers how these services handle a contributor's copyright, for example if you upload content to a service such as Facebook. Finally it will explore some of the copyright issues if you want to reuse material from one of these sites. Examples are included from some of the most popular Web 2.0 applications such as Flickr, Facebook and Wikipedia. The case study included in this chapter come from Zurich International School, where both primary and secondary school students (K-12) are encouraged to use Web 2.0 technologies in a responsible way that respects intellectual property.

What is Web 2.0?

It is worth briefly explaining what Web 2.0 technologies are, for the term was popularized in 2004 by the US media company O'Reilly Media, although it describes technologies that were developed in the 1990s. These technologies are sometimes called 'social software' as one of their features is usually the ability to share resources and communicate with other users across a network. Social software uses the internet as a platform to run software and services rather than a desktop PC, so most Web 2.0 tools are hosted remotely and can be accessed from anywhere with an internet connection. The online encyclopedia Wikipedia (which is itself social software) describes much of the background and definition of the term (Wikipedia, 2009). However, the use of the term has given rise to debate; for example Tim Berners-Lee, the 'inventor' of the world wide web dislikes the term 'Web 2.0', as he maintains that he always envisaged the web would allow people to collaborate and communicate in this way. He also argues that many supposed 'Web 2.0' technologies have existed since the beginnings of the internet and that the development of the 'Semantic web' (or Web 3.0) is far more significant. The Semantic web is the expression of web content not simply in natural language, but in 'a form that can be understood, interpreted and used by software agents, thus permitting them to find, share and integrate information more easily' (W3C, 2007).

While it is not necessary to debate terminology any further in this book, it is clear to many in education that the way we can interact with the internet has changed. If one examines the development of a website such as the BBC, over the last few years it is now far easier for users to contribute, share content and interact with this website. It is also clear that the concept of Web 2.0 has become mainstream and many of the tools and services such as RSS (Really Simple Syndication) feeds (a way of publishing rapidly changing web-based content), blogs and social networking sites are widely used. To summarize, some overall characteristics of social software or Web 2.0 include:

◆ development of social networks
◆ content created by users rather than created by an organization
◆ development of user profiles
◆ use of folksonomies, or tagging, to attach keywords created by users, to items to aid retrieval.

JISC has been a valuable source of advice relating to the use of Web 2.0 in education and associated copyright issues. In 2007 it highlighted six key concepts related to Web 2.0 technologies including: the creation of user-generated content, harnessing the power of the crowd, data on an epic scale, participation, network effects and openness (Anderson, 2007). What is apparent from these terms is that traditional modes of content creation, 'ownership' and most importantly copyright, do not sit well in the Web 2.0 world. When people write a document collaboratively on Wikipedia, it is not obvious who would own it. When people edit video material and upload it to YouTube, copyright issues are rarely considered. Many of these sites have an underlying ethos of sharing which is problematic in terms of copyright. Copyright laws specifically define who the author of a literary work is; however where work is created collaboratively using a Web 2.0 application such as a wiki the authorship is less clear. Anderson's report was particularly timely and provided the UK education community with a valuable overview of what Web 2.0 might be and how it might impact on education. However, it made just a brief mention of copyright issues.

In 2008 JISC funded a series of projects to explore how institutions might respond to 'emergent technologies'. It also produced a briefing paper entitled *Web 2.0 and Intellectual Property Rights* (JISC, 2008a) to highlight the key issues. It saw these as being:

◆ the collaborative nature of Web 2.0 – international multiple contributors who never meet will result in the shifting of risks, blurring of who owns copyright, who is responsible for dealing with infringements within different legal jurisdictions and/or the identity of collaborators
◆ consequential difficulties in policing and enforcing any infringements that might occur and establishing who is liable for what and when
◆ uncertainty about what may be permitted under exceptions to copyright, because of a lack of suitable case law (JISC, 2008a).

More recently, however, JISC reported on *Higher Education in a Web 2.0 World* (CLEX, 2009). Copyright issues were mentioned briefly in the context of young people having a 'casual approach' to copyright and other legal constraints. JISC also funded the Web2rights project (JISC, 2009) that provides a wealth of information and resources for further and higher education including an animation to highlight some of the key issues and an online diagnostic tool (JISC, 2008b). The project explored issues and questions such as:

◆ Do rights exist in a virtual world and, if so, who owns them?
◆ Who owns the rights in works that are a result of collective collaboration?
◆ What happens if you can't find the rights holders?
◆ What are the legal risks associated with Web 2.0 engagement?
◆ How can risks associated with content reuse be sensibly managed?

The project website has a valuable toolkit of resources for all sorts of possible scenarios. It also includes a diagnostic tool to help identify IPR and copyright issues. The IPR toolkit is reproduced in Figure 5.1.

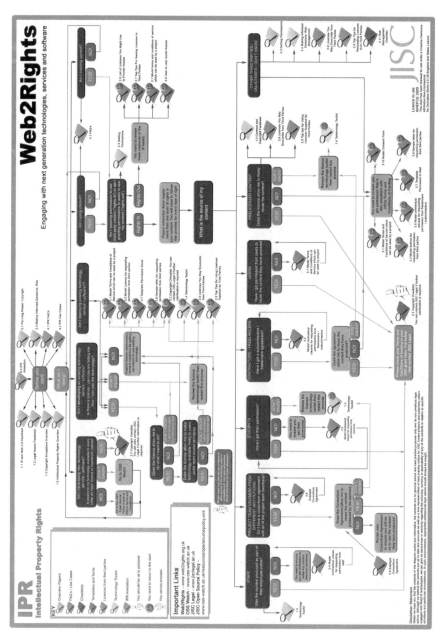

Figure 5.1
The Web2rights
IPR toolkit

This chapter will attempt to distil some of the advice from this project and from other organizations, however, this is unsurprisingly an area where technology is developing rapidly and the copyright laws are galloping to keep pace. Most recently, for example, The Digital Britain report (DCMS, 2009) highlighted the importance of copyright issues in relation to emerging technology. This report was discussed in more detail in Chapter 1 (see page 16), for it gave rise to the Digital Economy Act that went through the UK parliament in 2010. The government is committed to ensuring that the UK stays at the leading edge of the global digital economy and reforming some of our copyright laws were seen as central to achieving this aim. Therefore it seems likely that further changes will be made to UK copyright in the near future.

New technologies for learning

Since 2007 we have also seen an increasing number of improvements in both commercial and open-source e-learning systems to include Web 2.0 functionality.

The use of Web 2.0 technologies in higher education has led to some educational establishments relaxing their policy towards hosting data on third-party sites. Until recently, university IT departments steered away from such practices, recommending that data was kept on internal systems. However, many Web 2.0 commercial services provide tools and software that cannot easily be run in-house. In addition, many educational institutions are keen to engage with new technologies in response to student demands. This means that we are seeing an increasing amount of 'academic' content being hosted on third-party sites, such as Flickr, YouTube or Facebook, which has implications for copyright. However, this is not the case everywhere, and in other institutions, typically schools, further education colleges and in the health sector access to many Web 2.0 applications is blocked. In these institutions IT departments have taken the approach that the risks associated with using these services are too great to provide any educational benefit.

The risks associated with using Web 2.0 applications include:

◆ the security, privacy and data protection issues that uploading content to a third-party site might create

◆ concerns about retaining control of the intellectual outputs of an organization
◆ possible confusion if official branding or logos appear on third-party sites
◆ the staff time needed to manage these sites, for example moderating comments on a blog
◆ the copyright issues if staff or students upload content that infringes copyright or use infringing material from a Web 2.0 application
◆ the perception that many Web 2.0 applications are purely social sites and not appropriate to use in the workplace – Facebook is the most common site to be blocked by employers for this reason.

The risks aside, much has been written about the potential for Web 2.0 technologies to help engage learners, particularly younger students who have grown up with access to technologies such as mobile phones, computer games and the internet. Technologies such as blogs, social networking sites, wikis and podcasts are all being used widely, particularly in higher education at the present time. Meanwhile organizations such as JISC and Becta have been working to help ensure that educators and support staff have the appropriate skills to use these technologies effectively. This next section considers a number of these technologies and looks specifically at the copyright challenges they might present to both the staff who wish to use them and those in a teaching support role, such as librarians and learning technologists. There is considerable enthusiasm for experimentation in this field and many of the Web 2.0 tools encourage collaboration and content sharing. On the surface it appears that copyright issues are disregarded by both users and creators of many of these tools. The next section includes only a brief introduction to each technology, focusing on particular copyright issues associated with their use.

Blogs

Blogs or weblogs are essentially a website often in an online journal or diary format and usually written by a single named author who will upload entries or posts using a simple interface. They are arranged in reverse chronological order, with the most recent entry appearing at the top of the screen. Readers are provided with the ability to leave comments on the posts. A typical blog post is an opinion piece that might include links to resources and photos. Their value to the education community is considerable, particularly for teachers as a learning journal to aid reflection. There are numerous examples of blogs being used in teacher training, but some staff encourage students to use blogs to develop their writing and reflection skills. Blogging software can be installed on in-house servers or hosted externally and a number of commercial sites host blogs for free on behalf of users, such as Blogger.com (owned by Google) and WordPress.com.

Original blog entries are covered under copyright law, being original, fixed and authored by qualified nationals; therefore, permission to reuse entries should be sought even if a teacher has asked students to write a blog as part of their studies. Some bloggers use Creative Commons Licenses to highlight that they are happy for their entries to be reused. The licences can be attached to a personal blog, or staff can encourage their students to use one on their blog. Blogging is less likely to cause copyright issues from the author's perspective, if they stick to writing their entries as original opinion-based pieces. However, if the writer wishes to reproduce an entire entry or a substantial part of an entry from another blog then they are well advised to seek permission (as with any content you find on the internet) if there is not a Creative Commons License displayed. It is usual for bloggers to include their contact details or to have a commenting facility so getting permission is not difficult. Bloggers frequently write about and refer to other material on the internet. A good blog is likely to include links to other material on the internet, including reports, other blog posts by the same or other authors, or recent news stories. It is not usually necessary to seek permission to link to a post on another blog. If you wish to use photographs on your blog you are advised to use your own photos or to use photos with no copyright restrictions or those that are licensed under a Creative Commons License.

Blog services

Blogger (www.blogger.com) is a popular blog service owned by Google that allows people to set up a blog hosted remotely on external servers. The terms of use of the site include a section about intellectual property rights which clearly state that when using this site, the blog author retain copyright in their content (www.blogger.com/terms.g). The policy states:

> Google claims no ownership or control over any Content submitted, posted or displayed by you on or through Google services. You or a third-party licensor, as appropriate, retain all patent, trademark and copyright to any content you submit, post or display on or through Google services and you are responsible for protecting those rights, as appropriate.

This statement should reassure teachers who are concerned that by hosting their content on Blogger.com they will lose ownership of their data. In addition, as is common with many Web 2.0 technologies, Google encourage people to licence their content for reuse under a Creative Commons License.

WordPress is an open-source blog tool that offers both hosted blog services (http://wordpress.com) and allows users to download the software to it on their own servers (http://wordpress.org). For those educational establishments who feel uncomfortable about any content hosted on external sites, this latter option is useful. Like much open-source software, Wordpress is licensed under a GNU General Public Licence (a completely free software system compatible with Unix, www.gnu.org), which means that you are free to modify the source code. WordPress logos and graphics are available to use on your blog. The terms of service set out useful 'responsibilities for contributors' include the following:

> By making Content available, you represent and warrant that:
>
> - the downloading, copying and use of the Content will not infringe the proprietary rights, including but not limited to the copyright, patent, trademark or trade secret rights, of any third-party
> - if your employer has rights to intellectual property you create, you have either (i) received permission from your employer to post or make available the Content, including but not limited to any software, or (ii) secured from your employer a waiver as to all rights in or to the Content
> - you have fully complied with any third-party licences relating to

the Content, and have done all things necessary to successfully pass through to end users any required terms.

(WordPress, 2009)

Interestingly, the WordPress Terms of Service document is also licensed under a Creative Commons License, which explicitly states: 'You're more than welcome to steal it and repurpose it for your own use, just make sure to replace references to us with ones to you, and if you want we'd appreciate a link to WordPress.com somewhere on your site.'

Most virtual learning environments, for example Moodle and Blackboard, also now have in-built blogging tools that are password protected so only staff and students in the institution or on a course can view them, rather than them being freely available on the internet. While this does not mean that good practice in terms of copyright can be disregarded, password protecting blogs is seen as a way to reduce the risks associated with Web 2.0 tools. To avoid any potential problems, it is recommended best practice to include copyright advice as an integral part of any blog training whether it is a session for staff or for students, and regardless of whether the blog is publicly available or not. Many students might use a blog within a password protected VLE, but go on to set up a blog on a site such as WordPress or Blogger. Ensuring that they respect intellectual property should be part of any training programme.

Copyright advice for blog authors

Good practice advice for blog authors is summarized below:

◆ Blogs are usually opinion based, so writing an original piece that doesn't infringe copyright should be fairly straightforward if you stick to viewing your blog as your opinions and thoughts.
◆ Remember that what you write is publicly available on the internet, unless you password protect the site, so common sense should tell you not to write anything libellous about other people, your employer or companies.
◆ Link to other web-based materials you are referencing, but don't copy large amounts of material from other websites.
◆ If you wish to use photos on your blog, use your own photos, or find

photos that are licensed under a Creative Commons License and credit the original photographer.

◆ Protect your intellectual property with either a copyright symbol on your materials, or, if you are happy for the content to be used by others, a Creative Commons License attached.

Wikis

Wikis are an easy-to-edit website that allows content to be created collaboratively by multiple authors. They are particularly useful for group work and student projects, where several writers can work collaboratively to build up knowledge in an area. Wikis support version control, which means that changes can be tracked and earlier versions of a document can be retrieved even after a wiki has been published. In addition, individual contributions from different authors can be identified. However, wikis provide an interesting example in terms of copyright, because work is undertaken collaboratively and the content is often hosted on third-party sites. In terms of wikis that are used by staff as part of their employment, the content would be owned by the employer, as with any jointly authored piece of text. However, student work hosted on a wiki would be jointly owned by the group. If a tutor wishes to reuse the content from the wiki they would be advised, as with any piece of student work, to ask permission from the authors.

Wikipedia is the most well established and well known example of a wiki. Launched in 2000, it aimed to build an online encyclopaedia as the sum of all human knowledge. The Wikipedia software is called MediaWiki and it is licensed under a GNU General Public Licence for free download. This means that individuals and organizations are free to install the MediaWiki software on their own servers so that they can use it to set up their own wiki on any topic of interest. Again if the wiki is used by staff as part of their employment, it is no different to any other jointly authored document.

Wikipedia and copyright

Increasingly staff and students might want to contribute to Wikipedia and those who contribute to the site need to consider copyright issues carefully.

They should ensure that they do not submit any copyrighted material and that any content they include is their own original work. Cutting and pasting from elsewhere on the web to create a Wikipedia article infringes copyright and is not permitted in the terms of use, which specify you should only reuse content under a Creative Commons Attribution Share Alike Licence. Wikipedia also have a requirement that all material contributed to the site is re-licensed under this licence. The site states:

> All users contributing to Wikimedia projects are required to grant broad permissions to the general public to re-distribute and re-use their contributions freely, as long as the use is attributed and the same freedom to re-use and re-distribute applies to any derivative works. Therefore, for any text you hold the copyright to, by submitting it, you agree to license it under the Creative Commons Attribution/Share-Alike License 3.0.
>
> (Wikimedia Foundation, 2009)

Other wiki software

Increasingly, as with many Web 2.0 tools, free hosted wiki software is available to allow users to create wikis for their own use. Some examples of hosted wikis include PBWorks (http://pbworks.com) and WikiSpaces (www.wikispaces.com). A hosted wiki on the site PBWorks is still owned by the contributors, so PBWorks make no claims over ownership of what they term 'user submissions' in their Terms of Service. PBwiki also emphasize that material posted on their site should not infringe copyright. As is typical with many Web 2.0 services, copyright infringement is taken seriously and will result in suspension of a user's account. The terms of WikiSpaces are very similar to those of PBWiki. In addition, several virtual learning environments also include a wiki tool which could be used for a student project. These tools tend to have less functionality, but have the advantage of being password protected and restricted to students on a course of study. As is the case with blogs, password protection should not be viewed as a reason for infringing copyright when creating a wiki.

Good practice when using wikis

Good practice when using wikis includes:

◆ Considering the options carefully when deciding whether to use a hosted wiki on a third-party site, Wiki software hosted on your own servers, or a wiki tool available in your VLE or e-learning platform.

◆ Ensuring that copyright advice and the concept of Creative Commons are included in any technical training for wiki creation.

◆ If students are expected to use a wiki for a group project, remembering that the group will own the resulting project just as they would any other document.

Case Study 6: Zurich International School, New Zealand – e-learning and copyright

Mark Dilworth

Introduction

Zurich International School is a leading, non-profit day school offering a comprehensive education programme for students aged 2 to 18 in the greater Zurich and Baden areas. Over 1300 students from more than 45 countries attend one of the school's five campuses (Early Childhood Center in Kilchberg for students aged 2 to 5; Lower School in Wädenswil for students aged 5 to 11; Middle School in Kilchberg for students aged 11 to 14; Upper School in Adliswil for students aged 14 to 18; and ZIS Baden for students aged 2 to 12).

During the 2007–08 school year, ZIS began the transition of becoming a one-to-one laptop school. All teachers have received a Lenovo tablet computer and students in Grades 6–12 followed in 2008–09. All classrooms are equipped with interactive Smart Boards and wireless internet access is available throughout the campuses. Additional resources such as school e-mail, an e-learning platform and subscriptions to educational web services such as United Streaming (http://streaming.discoveryeducation.com) and Turnitin.com (http://turnitin.com) also support teaching and learning.

Web Portal and the VLE

The school's web portal has been designed to provide online and/or offsite access for all members of the school community while offering a range of curriculum delivery options for teachers and students depending on their needs. The resources that can be accessed from the web portal for student

Table 5.1 *List of resources available from the web portal for student learning*

VLE	Moodle
E-mail	Microsoft Exchange
Networked Folders	Shared Folders on File Server
Collaborative Calendars and Documents	Hosted Educational Google Apps
Blogs	Wordpress multi-user

learning are detailed in Table 5.1.

Teaching and learning

Teachers have worked hard to recognize the paradigm shift when working in a digital classroom. Classroom management has become an increasing priority for some teachers and professional development has focused on teaching and learning in the digital classroom. The school has also developed its e-learning platform using Moodle and other Web 2.0 tools to deliver curriculum. Teachers are integrating digital media with project-based learning in the form of video or audio components in culminating activities.

Students have quickly adapted themselves to the new learning environment. Their tablets have been imaged with a suite of programmes that include video, audio and image-editing tools. Many classes have gone paperless and students now create and submit all assignments digitally. Although it may vary from class to class, students have several options for collaborating and sharing their work using Networked Folders, Moodle Assignments, Blogs and Wikis or Google Apps.

The learning landscape at ZIS is changing. Supporting data from Google Analytics has confirmed a significant increase in traffic to ZIS's Moodle courses during the first year of the one-to-one programme. Circulation data from our Library has identified a decline in the use of traditional print media accompanying the introduction of digital equipment and resources to the library catalogue. Meanwhile, in the classroom, the internet is increasingly looked to as a source for research and curriculum content. ZIS supports these changes through faculty, resources and policy.

IT Curriculum Coordinators and Librarians work closely with the Principals to ensure that resources are adequate, policy is consistent and appropriate, and expectations of teachers and students are realistic. The library has seen its role shift from primarily providing traditional print resources to becoming a media centre for digital equipment and online resources. Students and teachers can sign out digital cameras, MP3 recorders, CDs and DVDs. Furthermore, IT Curriculum Coordinators and Librarians work together to support teachers with the integration of 21st Century skills into the curriculum.

With the onset of the tablet programme, it was decided that the IT department would shift its role from offering courses to supporting integration and, as such, there is no explicit IT Curriculum. Integration of IT skills is occurring across all subject areas to varying degrees. For example, integration does not always enhance learning in some courses offered through the Physical Education and Fine Arts Departments. Additionally, IT Curriculum Coordinators and the Librarians are working to promote and support the NETS-S (www.iste.org/Content/NavigationMenu/NETS/ForStudents/2007Standards/NETS_for_Students_2007.htm) as they are integrated across all curriculum areas. A purpose-built curriculum-mapping software is being populated by all teachers to provide a vertical and horizontal articulation of subject-specific curriculum in additional to identifying IT integration. Information from this software is then cross-referenced with data from the Atomic Learning Tech Skills Student Assessment (www.atomiclearning.com/k12/en/assessment) to identify areas of instructional need in Media Literacy and IT.

Students have many opportunities to select courses with a focus on media and IT-related content where discussions of copyright may arise. Computer Programming courses are available to students through participation in Virtual High School (VHS) (www.govhs.org). Video Journalism, Digital Design, and Digital Photography courses make full use of the Mac Lab to create and edit digital content. Music and Language courses employ digital tools and software to create audio content.

Increasing awareness of social networking is approached through parent sessions and student assemblies. The IT department hosts several parent and guardian sessions each year aimed at improving parent understanding of how students are using social networking and encouraging the discussions to continue at home. During school assemblies, students are made aware of the implications that social networking can have on their future education and professional careers. Students are recommended to consider how and what they are posting to the public domain as well as to monitor their privacy settings on any social networking sites they may use. Major policy changes to social networking sites such as Facebook are presented and explained so that students are cognizant of how these changes may affect them.

Policy

The Responsible Use Policy (RUP) aims to serve the evolving learning landscape and the intersection of education and copyright. It guides tablet and internet use in class, at school and on the network. The policy emphasizes an importance of copyright as it relates to education: 'I agree to comply with trademark, copyright laws, data protection laws and computer misuse laws, and to give credit to all sources used.'

The challenge to effectively implement this expectation is addressed in three ways.

First, ZIS is mapping its curriculum and this will facilitate linking curricular connections to media literacy and copyright awareness. Second, the RUP also includes *The Code of Best Practices in Media Literacy Education* (www. centerforsocialmedia.org/resources/publications/code_for_media_literacy_ education). These principles were created by the Center for Social Media to help educators and students using media literacy concepts and techniques to interpret the copyright doctrine of fair use. At ZIS, these principles are intended to guide best practice for the use of digital media in teaching and learning. Among other things, this can include the use of copyrighted materials as part of the curriculum and modifying pre-existing media objects in class works. Third, ZIS can publish student work online to blogs, YouTube and Flickr accounts. This is addressed in the RUP: 'Teachers and students publishing digital media to public sites as part of the curriculum should strive to ensure that they have the permission to share the content of their work and can apply a Creative Commons License to the work under an Attribution-NonCommercial-Share Alike licence.'

By applying Creative Commons Licenses to published student work, it encourages students to contribute to an increasing amount of web-based content that can be shared and drawn upon by others responsibly.

Conclusion

The ZIS Mission and Philosophy underpins the curriculum and its design, review, development and delivery. The ideas of Learn, Care, Challenge and Lead give the School the parameters to question what they teach and how they teach in a complex and ever-changing global environment. ZIS want their students to be active, rather than passive, learners who are critical and compassionate thinkers. They want them to be inspired and challenged to develop a love of learning, and to have this stay with them for the rest of their lives. Consequently learning about copyright issues is embedded into teaching and learning activities throughout the curriculum.

Media-sharing sites

Media sharing (such as photos, video and audio) is a feature of many Web 2.0 tools such as blogs and wikis. There are also numerous Web 2.0 sites designed specifically for sharing multimedia. Some of these have been discussed in Chapter 3 and they provide interesting examples in terms of their differing approaches to copyright. The two examples that will be explored in greater detail here are Flickr, which is predominantly a photo-sharing website, although videos can also be uploaded and YouTube, the video-sharing site. Both sites allow users to create a profile from which they can upload, organize and share content. The background and development of these two sites is explored in more detail, as well as their approaches to copyright. The chapter shows how these media-sharing sites have adopted differing approaches to copyright.

Flickr, http://flickr.com

Flickr is one of numerous media-sharing websites which allow users to upload content to share either with the wider public or to a restricted set of contacts. It was launched in 2004 by a Vancouver based company, although it has been owned by Yahoo since 2005. In October 2009, the site claimed to hold over four billion photographs (Flickr, 2009). The site is popular with many different types of users, from individuals who wish to share photos with friends to professional photographers showcasing their work. A free account allows the user to upload up to 200 photographs,

100MB of photographs and two videos per month, which can be tagged using keywords to facilitate searching. Users can also join groups where they are able to share photos related to specific topics. If you wish to upload more photographs then you need to upgrade your account to a 'Flickr Pro' account that has an annual subscription fee. The Pro account also allows you to upload more video files and organize your photographs in more sophisticated ways.

Organizations such as libraries and museums have started to use Flickr to showcase their photographic collections and the site allows content to be re-purposed to appear elsewhere on the web as a 'photostream'. There are a number of high profile libraries and museums in the world who now have a Flickr account, for example:

◆ The Library of Congress: ww.flickr.com/photos/library_of_congress
◆ The British Library: www.flickr.com/photos/britishlibrary
◆ The Metropolitan Museum of Art (New York): www.flickr.com/photos/metmuseum.

Most copyright laws in the world specify that the individual who takes a photograph owns the copyright of the resulting work. With the widespread availability of digital cameras large numbers of people can easily create content in the form of digital photographs. In addition, many mobile phones now have integral cameras that enable photographs and short video footage to be captured. Photo and video-sharing has become increasingly popular as sending files via e-mail can be problematic due to large file sizes. To respect copyright, the default option when uploading a photograph to Flickr is to protect the rights of the owner and label it as 'All rights reserved' meaning that permission must be sought if someone wishes to copy that image. However, a small but increasing number of individuals and organizations are licensing their photograph collections on Flickr to indicate that they are happy to allow reuse. Flickr's use of Creative Commons Licenses is discussed in greater detail in the following section.

Flickr's terms of use specify that you must own the copyright of any photographs that are uploaded to the site and that they reserve the right to remove anything they consider inappropriate or infringing. However, in general the ownership of photographic collections is relatively unproblematic in terms of copyright. Digital photography has led professionals in this area to use DRM to control who uses their photographs. For example, some professional photographers use techniques such as watermarking to safeguard their copyright. Others make only low resolution copies of photographs publicly available and charge a fee to download the higher resolution version. Matters can also become more complicated if individuals take photographs of copyright protected works, such as paintings or other works of art. If you acquire digital photographs that you did not take yourself you are strongly advised not to upload these to a photo-sharing website such as Flickr. If you wish to digitize photographs from a historical collection you should also remember that copyright protection in the UK is awarded to photographs for 70 years after the death of the author (that is, the person who took the photo). Also remember that even if you commissioned a photograph, you do not own the copyright, the photographer does by default.

Flickr and Creative Commons

Flickr has done considerable work to encourage the sharing and reuse of photographs under licences such as Creative Commons Attribution Share Alike. The Creative Commons search has an embedded Flickr image search that allows you to identify photographs licensed for reuse. It is also possible to search Flickr and limit your search to specific types of Creative Commons Licenses. So, for example, those looking for images that can be reused for commercial purposes will find a large bank of photographs on the site. The concept of Creative Commons has gained wider publicity through association and embedding within the Flickr website. Arguably Flickr is an example of a Web 2.0 service that has raised awareness of copyright issues and helped to build up good practice in terms of reusing content.

YouTube, http://youtube.com

YouTube is a video-sharing website that was launched in 2005 by three former PayPal employees. It was bought by Google in November 2006 and has rapidly became one of the most popular sites on the internet. It incorporates many Web 2.0 features such as the user profile (called a channel), tagging to facilitate access, commenting and ratings. With a strap line of 'broadcast yourself' the site capitalizes on increased ease of creating and editing video-recordings without sophisticated hardware and software. In addition, an increasing number of media companies and large organizations are using YouTube to host some of their content. However, it is often the user-generated content in the form of the home video that is enormously popular. The ability to create digital video clips, for example using a digital still camera or a mobile phone, has meant that many people can easily create digital video files. By using a video-sharing site such as YouTube individuals can easily share this content with others via the internet. Additionally, use of video editing software makes copying digital video from a DVD or from the internet relatively straightforward. It is here that the copyright issues become more serious and the entertainment and music industries have been working extremely hard to shut down illegal file sharing sites that threaten their business models.

YouTube is one of the most popular Web 2.0 sites, being populated largely by 'user-generated content' much of which is created by people using simple recording equipment, sometimes no more sophisticated than a mobile phone. However YouTube is probably the site that epitomizes the problematic relationship advocates of Web 2.0 technologies have with modern copyright laws. The site has been littered with examples of blatant copyright infringement, whereby individuals have copied copyright protected works, such as commercial video or DVD recordings, live performances and audio content. The allegations of copyright infringement were so frequent that YouTube amended their copyright policies and now take steps to demonstrate that they are taking copyright infringement seriously. This is done largely through their copyright notice which sets out how to make a complaint of copyright infringement and is available online at YouTube Copyright Infringement Notification: www.youtube.com/t/copyright_notice, and YouTube Copyright Tips: www.youtube.com/t/howto_copyright.

YouTube also provide Copyright Tips designed to educate users about how to avoid infringement. These set out what copyright is, how to identify copyright works, what the penalties might be if you upload copyright work (your account could be closed and you could be sued). They offer the following helpful advice:

The way to ensure that your video doesn't infringe someone else's copyright is to use your skills and imagination to create something completely original. It could be as simple as taping some of your friends goofing around, and as complicated as filming your own short movie with a script, actors, and the whole works. If it's all yours, you never have to worry about the copyright—you own it!

(YouTube, 2009)

They go on to warn users that even the audio should be original and that: 'if you use an audio track of a sound recording owned by a record label without that record label's permission, your video may be infringing the copyrights of others, and may be subject to removal'.

Users also see the following message at the time of uploading their video, although content is not routinely screened before uploading takes place:

Do not upload any TV shows, music videos, music concerts or commercials without permission unless they consist entirely of content you created yourself. The Copyright Tips page and the Community Guidelines can help you determine whether your video infringes someone else's copyright.

(YouTube, 2009)

YouTube rely on their users to alert them to inappropriate content and the site is hosted in the United States and therefore the copyright law cited is US Copyright Law, where fair use could be argued. Case law has shown that the removal of content from YouTube for copyright infringement is not always straightforward despite their stated policy. In August 2008 in the case Lenz vs Universal Music Corp. the court ruled that a copyright owner cannot order an online file to be removed from a video-sharing site without first determining if it was fair use. The woman in question Stephanie Lenz had made a home video of her young son dancing to a Prince song and had posted the video on YouTube.

YouTube and e-learning

Complaints continue that YouTube contains inappropriate content and that relying on users to flag inappropriate material, rather than routinely screening the site as content is uploaded, is irresponsible. In some countries access to YouTube is blocked and in many schools this is also the case. Nevertheless, YouTube is being used by increasing numbers in the education community as a platform to host educational materials, as well as a source for teachers to find relevant content produced by others. YouTube's education channel (YouTube EDU: www.youtube.com/ channels?s=ytedu_mv) was launched in March 2009 and universities in the United States, UK and elsewhere are using YouTube to distribute some of their content. YouTube has several advantages as a platform for hosting video content, provided educational establishments take steps to ensure that their content does not infringe copyright. For example, it can be a useful way of getting wider publicity for training or promotional materials for an institution. It also offers storage space for high quality video content that would otherwise need to be placed on an institutional streaming server.

In terms of using YouTube as a source of content for teaching, it can be more problematic than other sources due to the possibility of some content-infringing copyright laws. Teachers would be well advised not to rely on video content from YouTube being available long after they first access it as it can be removed with little or no warning. Fortunately, unlike photo-sharing sites, YouTube does not encourage (or make it easy) to download videos, so that linking to resources is the safest way for a teacher to share content with students. YouTube content can be embedded into a variety of other platforms such as blogs and social networking sites relatively easily. Using the 'share' option users can obtain a link to a video and once you have a YouTube account you can bookmark resources and also obtain a piece of Hypertext Markup Language (HTML) code to embed the video into a website or virtual learning environment. There is also a PowerPoint add-on which allows teachers to embed a YouTube video into their slideshow that does not require the file to be downloaded from the YouTube site.

Good advice for those using YouTube in teaching is as follows:

♦ As with all content on the web, be discerning about who produced the video, if it is good quality and if it is likely to infringe copyright.
♦ If you are encouraging students to create content for uploading to YouTube, ensure that they follow good practice in terms of not infringing copyright and give them guidance about where they can source music for their production.

◆ Explore the YouTube EDU site and also TeacherTube (www.teachertube.com) which contains educational videos (check out more resources in Chapter 3).

File sharing

The music and movie industries have the most problematic relationship with new technologies when it comes to copyright. The rise of internet technologies in the 1990s and the development of MP3 format, led many enterprising individuals to exploit these technologies for 'file sharing'. File sharing in itself is not illegal, however, the unauthorized sharing of copyright protected works (such as music or films) is illegal. There are few who are not familiar with the case of the original Napster website, which was eventually shut down following legal challenges from the music industry. The industry has done much to regulate how we access music over the internet and more importantly, how we pay for it. There are several legal music-sharing websites, the most famous of which is iTunes. It is sufficient to say that file sharing of copyright works using an e-learning platform would constitute a copyright infringement and that those wanting to use multimedia in teaching are advised to read Chapter 3. In addition the Conclusion contains a list of additional resources for teachers.

Social networking sites

Social networking sites were first launched in 2002, with the appearance of sites such as Friendster (www.friendster.com) and MySpace (www.myspace.com). They have become enormously popular in recent years with growing numbers of people throughout the world. Social networking sites are another example of Web 2.0 technology, allowing individuals to create a profile to communicate with both real friends and new contacts with similar interests. Users can upload content such as photos and videos to social networks, create and join groups and share resources with each other. Facebook (www.facebook.com) rapidly became the social network of choice amongst the higher education community in the US and UK, after its launch in 2005. It started life as a site for Harvard students in 2003, but after first extending membership to other universities, it was opened to the world in 2007. In February 2009 it was reported that 175 million people use Facebook. Meanwhile other social networking sites are aimed at the professional sector, for example LinkedIn (www.linkedin.com) is a professional networking site, used in some areas of business.

In terms of copyright, there are several issues to be aware of when using social networking sites. It pays to scrutinize the terms and conditions of any Web 2.0 site, but individuals should be particularly wary of social networking sites, which inevitably contain a lot of personal information. Some teachers have used social networking sites such as Facebook or Ning (www.ning.com) for teaching purposes. The recent JISC report on Higher education in a Web 2.0 world (JISC, 2009) recognized the engaging nature of social networking sites, which is often in contrast to more formal learning spaces such as VLEs. Nevertheless they should be approached with caution if they are going to be used for teaching purposes. In addition, most social networks are hosted by external companies, which mean that personal data about students and teachers is shared with a third-party. It would be unwise to compel students to use third-party services given that some students may feel uncomfortable with the terms and conditions of these sites. There are also several free open-source social networking tools that can be downloaded and several universities host their own social networking to retain ownership of what is often highly personal data. Probably the most widely used of these is Elgg (http://elgg.com). The disadvantage is that students may be reluctant to join a social networking site for their study, in addition to using a VLE. In this next section we'll look specifically at the copyright issues of both Facebook and Twitter (http://twitter.com) which many have come to regard as a social networking site.

Facebook

The Facebook terms and conditions have received widespread publicity recently, as the site updated its privacy policy several times in 2009. However, the site has a clearly stated copyright policy that sets out how to report any copyright infringement (Facebook, 2009a). Their terms and conditions also state that:

- You will not post content or take any action on Facebook that infringes or violates someone else's rights or otherwise violates the law.
- We can remove any content or information you post on Facebook if we believe that it violates this Statement.
- We will provide you with tools to help you protect your intellectual property rights.

(Facebook, 2009b)

Facebook allow users to appeal if their content is removed on the grounds that it infringes someone else's copyright and they believe that this was a mistake. However if you repeatedly infringe other people's intellectual property rights then your account will be disabled.

In line with many other sites that rely on 'user-generated content', there is a risk that when an individual uploads content to Facebook, they may be infringing the copyright of another. In terms of an individual user's copyright, Facebook has recently backtracked on an amendment to its terms and conditions with regard to ownership of user data, including personal photographs. In early February 2009 it was widely reported in the UK media (*The Times*, 2009) that Facebook intended to assert copyright in all content (for example, photographs, messages) that users uploaded to their site, even if users cancelled their account. By 2009 Facebook was being used by over 175 million people worldwide, with many working in the higher education sector – a group of people who might arguably have had a greater understanding of intellectual property law. Many individuals had uploaded personal content such as photos and videos to Facebook to share with friends and relatives. The idea that a private company would now own the copyright of this content was therefore a matter of great concern. After widespread protests, this policy was withdrawn several weeks later and the old terms and conditions were reinstated.

In terms of their value to teaching, social networking sites have many advantages over traditional e-learning systems in terms of engaging students. Sites such as Facebook have also developed robust policies in terms of protecting themselves against allegations of copyright infringement. These policies could provide useful models for the e-learning community, as they also provide examples of how to 'police' a site which allows users to upload potentially infringing material.

Twitter, http://twitter.com

Although described by many as a 'micro-blogging' site, Twitter has much in common with a social network and has several applications in an educational context. It was launched in 2006 and has attracted considerable media attention not least because of the large number of celebrities who use it. Based around the idea of sharing 'status updates', users register with the site, create a limited profile and then start posting updates. Posts are limited to 140 characters, so rather than overwhelm people with information, Twitter can be a fast and simple way of finding out what people are doing or what topics are making the news. You can choose to 'follow' people, or you can search the site for words or tags which are indicated with the # symbol. Twitter can be a useful way of sharing links to web-based resources and photos can also be uploaded to Twitter. The Terms of Service are clear that users retain the copyright of any content they post to Twitter but:

> By submitting, posting or displaying Content on or through the Services, you grant us a worldwide, non-exclusive, royalty-free license (with the right to sublicense) to use, copy, reproduce, process, adapt, modify, publish, transmit, display and distribute such Content in any and all media or distribution methods (now known or later developed).
>
> (Twitter, 2009)

Twitter also have a Copyright policy listed under the terms of service, which asks that you respect others intellectual property when using their service. It sets out how to report any allegations of copyright infringement and warns users that if they infringe copyright then they will have their content removed and repeat offenders may have their account withdrawn. Twitter is an interesting Web 2.0 example that has led some (Bailey, 2008; Cuban 2009) to question whether 'tweets' can be copyrighted given the 140 character restriction. Bailey suggests that the likelihood of copyright infringement on Twitter is also very low. However, in the absence of any relevant case law those in education using

Twitter would be well advised to treat it like any other blogging service in terms of copyright for the time being.

Social bookmarking sites

Social bookmarking tools are particularly useful for individuals to manage their resources. Instead of using browser-based Favourites or Bookmarks, links to useful websites can be 'bookmarked' on a website such as Delicious. As is common with many Web 2.0 tools, users create a profile and then store their favourites online, meaning that they are accessible from anywhere with an internet connection. They can also be shared with others and searched. In general, most copyright laws recognize that linking to another website cannot by classed as copyright infringement and is a fundamental part of the web. There are general good practice guidelines about how to avoid 'passing off' another's content as your own, such as avoiding frame links, but social bookmarking sites can be used in education largely without any concerns about infringing copyright. Educators who wish to keep their bookmarks private may prefer not to use a social bookmarking site.

Delicious, http://delicious.com

The Delicious copyright policy is part of the wider copyright and intellectual property rights statements provided by its parent company Yahoo, which took over the site in December 2005. There are no specific copyright issues associated with using a social bookmarking site such as Delicious and a user cannot claim copyright in a set of internet bookmarks.

Diigo, www.diigo.com

Diigo is a slightly different type of social bookmarking tool to Delicious, in that as well as allowing you to bookmark and organize your favourites, it also allows you to annotate and archive the material you find useful on the web, on a Diigo server. Under UK law, storing even temporary copies of web pages was until 2003 technically illegal. However, Diigo is a US-based service and operates under the fair use provision in the US Copyright Act. A user of this site in the UK might similarly be able to claim 'fair dealing' if they are using the site for private non-commercial research or study. In terms of their policy towards copyright they state:

> You may not post, modify, distribute, or reproduce in any way any copyrighted material, trademarks, or other proprietary information belonging to others without obtaining the prior written consent of the owner of such proprietary rights. It is the policy of Diigo.com to terminate Membership privileges of any Member who repeatedly infringes the copyright rights of others upon receipt of prompt notification to Diigo.com by the copyright owner or the copyright owner's legal agent.

In addition they have a clear policy on how to proceed if you believe that your copyright has been infringed by a Diigo user. Interestingly, Diigo have a group for those interested in copyright issues with a useful set of bookmarks: http://groups.diigo.com/group/rl-copyright.

Zotero, www.zotero.org

Zotero is a free Firefox plug-in which allows you to store references online. It works in a similar way to reference management software such as Endnote and RefWorks. The latest version of Zotero also allows users to store their PDF files and it is increasingly being used by students in higher education as an alternative to proprietary reference management software. Again the software was developed in the United States where copyright law includes the concept of fair use, but fair dealing in the UK also permits copies of materials to be stored for private study or research. Fundamentally this tool is a personal reference management tool and therefore any references including the full text are stored in a personal library, rather than a public archive. This means that there are no real copyright implications of using this software in teaching.

Virtual worlds

This chapter now briefly considers copyright issues associated with using virtual worlds, which are sometimes called multi-user environments. Virtual worlds are one of the emerging technologies that the JISC and

Eduserv have been exploring in relation to how they can be used in education (Kirriemuir, 2009). Second Life and Open Sim are the most commonly used virtual worlds in higher education and both are immersive environments where users 'create avatars (physical personas), meet, trade, communicate and develop (virtual) infrastructures in a shared online environment' (Kirriemuir, 2009).

Second Life is being used in educational establishments around the world and for a variety of purposes including: to hold meetings and classes, for student exhibitions, to facilitate distance learning, for student recruitment, online research and dissemination. Much of the use of virtual worlds is still experimental and it tends to require a high specification computer to operate. However, these environments are an area of growing interest to the e-learning community. Those who wish to use a virtual world, be they teachers or students, are well advised to familiarize themselves with the terms and conditions that govern their use.

Second Life

Second Life is a multi-user virtual world created by a company called Linden Labs and launched in 2003. While virtual worlds are different to the real world, copyright laws need to be respected and users should also respect trademarks and other intellectual property rights in this environment. Second Life has a clear policy in terms of ownership of content that is added to their site. While you retain the copyright of your content, by uploading it to the site, you are granting Linden Labs a royalty free licence to reuse your content as they see fit. Further details are available in their Terms of Service (Second Life, 2009). Some have argued that taking screen-shots from Second Life as a visitor could infringe the copyright of the creator.

Copyright theft is not uncommon in Second Life and cases need to be pursued through real world courts. The first case of copyright infringement in Second Life was in 2007 [*EROS vs John Doe*] although there was considerable concern in 2006 about the creation of the 'Copybot' software, which was subsequently outlawed. As a website hosted in the US, the copyright policy for using Second Life refers to US legislation, specifically the Digital Millennium Copyright Act. The terms of service set out clearly that users should not infringe copyright when adding content to Second

Life. The procedure for reporting potential copyright infringement is also set out in the terms of use, and Linden Labs state that any infringing content will be removed until a counter notification is filed. The policy also protects trademarks and other intellectual property rights. The company's takedown policy means that a user who believes that their content, which is often code, has been stolen can file a takedown notice. However, in reality it can be problematic to police this as content can easily be re-uploaded elsewhere in Second Life. Educators using Second Life should avoid infringing copyright, but also be aware that protecting their investment, such as any new content that they build, might be problematic.

Other trends

Two other trends that are worth briefly considering in terms of how they relate to copyright are the rise of what has been called 'cloud computing' and also mobile learning. Gartner (2008) defines cloud computing as 'a style of computing where massively scalable IT-related capabilities are provided "as a service" using internet technologies to multiple external customers'. In practice it can mean that an organization might choose to outsource some of its IT provision. In 2009 in higher education we have seen several universities choose to outsource their e-mail to Google, rather than running a mail service internally. Cloud computing solutions mean that the education sector needs to become more aware of IPR issues to ensure that any contracts with third-party suppliers specify that the ownership of data lies with the institution and not with the service provider.

Mobile learning is another growing trend where institutions are working with mobile phone suppliers to develop applications that allow their data to be delivered to handheld devices. For example, several universities have worked with Apple to develop iPhone applications. In terms of copyright, the ownership of the data again needs to be considered. As we saw with the University of Oxford iTunes U case study, the institution ensured that ownership of the resulting material was retained.

Conclusion

There are a number of common issues with regard to emerging

technologies and how they protect both an individual's copyright and the copyright of others. Many of the Web 2.0 services and tools are in fact now owned by one of the large internet companies (such as Google or Yahoo) and have well established copyright and privacy policies in addition to detailed terms and conditions of use. At the same time as these services are evolving, e-learning practitioners are struggling to manage the online behaviour of teachers or students who are less familiar with copyright law. Staff often feel uncomfortable acting as a 'policing' body over what can and cannot be uploaded into a virtual learning environment. This chapter on Web 2.0 services highlights that by putting the responsibility onto the individual, through clearly stated terms of use, many Web 2.0 sites could serve as a model for the education world as to how we police our virtual learning environments.

Currently, education seems to perceive that responsibility lies with an institution to inform teachers about copyright law. In fact, if educational establishments were to devise policies and terms of use for their e-learning system, then all staff that sign up to use the VLE would take personal responsibility for copyright issues. This would mean that copyright would become a matter for individuals and the claim that 'no one told me about copyright restrictions' would be difficult to maintain. If an individual were to post an infringing video-recording onto YouTube and then maintain that no one at YouTube gave them a training session telling them that they could not do this, the argument would be clearly flawed. E-learning staff grappling with emerging technologies might consider the approach of many Web 2.0 service providers and adopt a similar attitude to managing copyright in online learning.

References

Andersen (2007) *What is Web 2.0? Ideas, Technologies and Implications for Education. JISC Technology and Standards Watch*, www.jisc.ac.uk/media/documents/techwatch/tsw0701b.pdf [accessed 8 January 2010].

Bailey, J. (2008, 5 May) *Copyright and Twitter*, the Blog Herald, www.blogherald.com/2008/05/05/copyright-and-twitter [accessed 8 January 2010].

CLEX (2009) *Higher Education in a Web 2.0 World*, Committee of Inquiry

into the Changing Learner Experience,
www.jisc.ac.uk/media/documents/publications/heweb20rptv1.pdf
[accessed 12 February 2010].

Cornish, G. (2009) *Copyright: interpreting the law for libraries, archives and information services*, 5th edn, Facet Publishing.

Cuban, M. (2009) *Are Tweets Copyrighted?* Blog Maverick,
http://blogmaverick.com/2009/03/29/are-tweets-copyrighted
[accessed 17 December 2009].

DCMS (2009) *Digital Britain: the final report*,
www.culture.gov.uk/what_we_do/broadcasting/6216.aspx [accessed 10 January 2010].

Facebook, (2009a) *Facebook Copyright Policy*,
www.facebook.com/legal/copyright.php [accessed 8 January 2010].

Facebook, (2009b) *Terms of Use*,
www.facebook.com/terms.php?ref=pf [accessed 8 January 2010].

Flickr (2009, 12 October) *4,000,000,000*, Flickr Blog,
http://blog.flickr.net/en/2009/10/12/4000000000 [accessed 8 January 2010].

Gartner (2008) *Gartner Says Cloud Computing will be as Influential as e-Business*, Gartner Press release,
www.gartner.com/it/page.jsp?id=707508 [accessed 10 January 2010].

Kirriemuir, J. (2009) *Virtual World Watch: surveying virtual world use in UK universities and college*,
http://virtualworldwatch.net [accessed 18 December 2009].

Ofcom (2009) *Estimated Take-up of Broadband Services, By Country*,
www.ofcom.org.uk/research/stats/bb_takeup.pdf [accessed 10 January 2010].

JISC (2008a, 2 April) *Web 2.0 and Intellectual Property Rights*. JISC Briefing paper,
www.jisc.ac.uk/publications/documents/bpweb20iprv1.aspx
[accessed 8 January 2010].

JISC (2008b) *Web2Rights Diagnostic Tool*,
www.web2rights.org.uk/diagnostic.html [accessed 8 January 2010].

JISC (2009) *Web2rights*,
www.web2rights.org.uk [accessed 8 January 2010].

Second Life (2009) *Terms of Service*,
http://secondlife.com/corporate/tos.php [accessed 8 January 2010].

The Times (2009, 18 Feb) Users Force Facebook to Withdraw Controversial 'Copyright' Plan, http://technology.timesonline.co.uk/tol/news/tech_and_web/article57 57485.ece [accessed 8 January 2010].

Twitter (2009) *Terms of Service*, http://twitter.com/tos [accessed 8 January 2010].

W3C (2007). *W3C Semantic Web Frequently Asked Questions*, World Wide Web Consortium, www.w3.org/2001/sw/SW-FAQ#What1 [accessed 10 January 2010].

Wikimedia Foundation (2009) *Terms of Use*, http://wikimediafoundation.org/wiki/Terms_of_Use [accessed 8 January 2010].

Wikipedia (2009) *Web 2.0*, http://en.wikipedia.org/wiki/Web_2.0 [accessed 8 January 2010].

WordPress (2009) *Terms of Service*, http://en.wordpress.com/tos/ [accessed 8 January 2010].

YouTube (2009) *YouTube: copyright tips*, www.youtube.com/t/howto_copyright [accessed 12 February 2010].

6

Copyright training for staff

Introduction

As the digital learning environment develops, it is becoming increasingly important for educational institutions to offer some form of copyright training for teachers, lecturers, administrative staff and researchers. It may also be an area that students will need educating about as part of wider digital literacy skills. The implications of infringing the rights of others in the electronic environment are far greater than in the classroom and activities that once took place face-to-face are far more visible and permanent in a digital space. In addition, as we have seen in Chapter 4, it is far easier to make a perfect 'copy' of a digital work and to distribute it to many others without realizing the legal implications that follow. A range of external bodies, for example, professional bodies for librarians such as the Chartered Institute of Library and Information Professionals (CILIP) and Aslib have offered copyright training courses for many years. In addition, other organizations offer copyright training that focuses on particular types of resources; for example JISC Digital Media offer copyright courses for those producing multimedia content. However, often the most cost-effective and efficient means of delivering training to large groups of staff will be through offering an in-house training programme. In addition, many courses may be suitable for particular groups of staff, such as library staff, but might not be appropriate for teaching or administrative staff. In this chapter, the set up and organization of a copyright training programme is outlined. The chapter also identifies suitable resources to support staff who are delivering the training in your organization. The case study comes from the London School of Economics and Political Science and outlines how copyright training is dealt with in this institution.

A range of other organizations offer copyright training, including a number of independent consultants who work in this area. For example, bodies such as the Association of Learned and Professional Society Publishers (ALPSP) offer courses for those working in the publishing industry. Specialist organizations such as the British Universities Film and Video Council (BUFVC) also offer copyright courses designed for those dealing with video and audio material. For a full list of copyright training providers see the Conclusion of the book. While external courses are valuable, clearly it is not desirable or cost effective to send large numbers of staff in one institution on external training. However, it is essential that those involved in teaching using an online learning environment be given a thorough overview of copyright in order that they understand what they can and cannot do from a legal perspective. For this reason, being able to offer in-house copyright training should form an important component in any organization's staff development provision.

This chapter outlines the necessary steps to be taken when devising an in-house copyright training programme, by first considering the selection of a suitable trainer and the preparation that they might require. In cases where there is an institutional Copyright Officer, the selection process may be straightforward; however in other institutions it may be more appropriate for a number of staff to be up-skilled in order that they might deliver a copyright programme. Second, the chapter goes on to examine the intended audience of the training programme, the method of training, including face-to-face teaching versus using online learning. Finally it looks at developing support materials, such as booklets or guides and strategies for dealing with the host of queries that copyright issues inevitably lead to.

The copyright trainer

Deciding who should deliver copyright training may be a straightforward matter in institutions where there is a designated Copyright Officer who has responsibility for advice and support in relation to such matters. However in many smaller organizations, such as further education colleges, schools or in public sector or charitable organizations this sort of role is very rare. In fact, many people reading this book may well be doing so because of the absence of a Copyright Officer in their institution. The decision to create such a post is not taken lightly, due to the knowledge and experience such as post requires, however institutions are urged to consider establishing such a post, or ensuring that one or more dedicated members of staff have responsibility for copyright issues written into their job descriptions. The case study in Chapter 1 provides an example of how one institution, Brunel University in the UK, deals with copyright issues through a dedicated post.

In many smaller educational establishments the resources to establish a dedicated Copyright Officer will not be available. If this in the case, then it is recommended that one or more individuals should be trained in more depth so that they might take responsibility for copyright including providing training and advice within the institution. In some instances this responsibility may fall on a member of staff within the library or learning resources centre, who may be responsible for signing and managing licences for electronic resources. However, other institutions will consider it more appropriate that a senior member of administrative staff should take on this responsibility. Some institutions may have a legal compliance team who deal with issues such as Data Protection and Freedom of Information requests. Copyright and IPR issues often sit naturally with these responsibilities. Whoever decides to take on responsibility for copyright, whether it be one or more persons, while they do not need to be legally qualified they should have:

◆ A good overview of the appropriate copyright laws of their respective country – there are both courses and books that provide an excellent grounding and these are listed at the end of this book.
◆ Familiarity with licences in the digital environment for subscription resources but also freely available digital resources and some knowledge of the emerging e-copyright environment, such as Creative Commons.
◆ A support mechanism for referring questions that goes beyond their knowledge or understanding. In higher education in the UK JISCLegal Services and membership of the JISCmail list LIS-copyseek, where queries can be routed, might be sufficient to cover this.

Finally it is highly recommended that more than one person has a good working knowledge of copyright in order to cover staff absences, ensure a reasonable workload and to provide different perspectives on an issue.

Developing a copyright training programme

As we have seen in earlier chapters, the widespread use of VLEs and other e-learning systems in education, mean that it is far easier for staff to inadvertently infringe copyright and claim, quite legitimately, that they did not know they were doing anything wrong. Most institutions are starting to invest significantly in training programmes that provide staff with the technical skills they need to create and upload content into an online learning space. While, there is no formal requirement to offer in-house copyright training alongside the technical training, it is recommended as best practice. In addition, those in the UK Higher Education sector who have a Copyright Licensing Agency Licence should ideally have a training programme in place. For while copyright training is not mentioned specifically in the terms of the CLA HE Licence, part of the requirements of the licence are for institutions to be audited about their scanning procedures. The checklist used during a CLA Audit (CLA, 2009) looks for evidence that staff and students in the institutions receive guidance and training about the licence and copyright more generally. It also looks for evidence about how an institution communicates to its student population about restrictions on scanning, and how they pursue infringing the use of copyright-protected material by academic staff and students.

Aside from any legal obligations, providing a copyright training programme should form an essential component of a rounded staff development provision. Institutions who do not offer any copyright training would be well advised to undertake a risk assessment to explore the possible implications of a copyright infringement claim. In the worst case scenario a rights holder, for example a large publisher, might decide to pursue a case of copyright infringement. By having a training programme in place this could act as a valuable defence in court. Institutions which can demonstrate that all staff received copyright training would be better placed, with the onus being on the individual who carried out that infringement, rather than negligence on the part of the organization. That said, it is standard practice in many organizations for staff contracts or terms and conditions to explicitly state that during the course of their employment staff must not infringe copyright. This is also often part of the conditions of use associated with computer technology in many organizations. This places the responsibility onto individual members of staff, yet in any organization, without adequate support and advice in place, staff may be inclined to blame their employers if they think that they have not been given appropriate guidance. Moreover, in preparing e-learning materials, teaching staff may also implicate other staff members, such as learning support staff or administrative staff if issues such as copyright are not flagged up during a training session.

Embedding copyright training in the institution

Once the decision has been taken to provide a copyright training programme, some thought should be given to the method of delivery. Standalone copyright courses inevitably suffer from poor attendance, with many teaching staff viewing it as a low priority to learn about such matters. Some staff actively avoid attending courses such as this, with the attitude 'I'll probably be told about lots of things I can't do.' Therefore it is essential to develop a range of carefully targeted (and well publicized) courses in addition to online support materials. Wherever possible these courses and associated materials should avoid legal jargon and be written in a 'what you need to know' style, for example including frequently asked questions about copyright issues. By providing a suite of copyright support, organizations go some way towards protecting themselves from possible litigation. Offering training to new staff (particularly new teachers) is also key, but an embedded approach to copyright training is often the most successful approach, where copyright advice is offered during technical hands-on training sessions that teachers using the VLE attend. For example, offering a course about how to use images in teaching, but including within that course advice and guidance about how to find copyright-free images. This raises the issue of copyright, but does so in the context of a positive activity that members of staff will find helpful for their teaching. In this case staff may want to illustrate their lecture slides using images, so the focus can be on good sources of images that can be reused (such as those in free image banks, or images licensed using Creative

Commons). More details about sources of copyright-free image collections are available in Chapter 3.

In developing your copyright programme you should think about the training courses currently on offer at your institution and whether it might be relevant to embed some copyright advice into these courses; for example, a course about creating a website, or uploading resources to the VLE, could remind staff that they should only use material where they own the copyright or else they will need to obtain permission. It is useful in this process to undertake a training audit and speak to as many people as possible about the training and advice that they currently provide to staff. If you have an in-house staff development unit then this will be a good place to start for a list of courses. If your institution does not have a dedicated staff development team, you may find that training is offered by various departments such as the IT department, the Library, the e-learning team and any teaching and learning support, such as teacher training programmes.

Your audience: training staff members

When devising your programme it will be helpful to divide staff into different categories in order to tailor the training to specific audience needs. What a person needs to know about copyright and the level of detail of that knowledge will vary significantly depending on their role. For example, the type of training a departmental administrator will need might vary considerably from that of a researcher, and teaching staff have specific requirements which differ from those who work in the finance department. In many cases rolling out copyright training to all staff is going to be difficult and it may need to concentrate on specific groups where the needs are greatest. The staff to target in the first instance might include:

◆ library staff
◆ learning support staff/educational developers/learning technologists
◆ reprographic unit staff
◆ departmental administrators/secretaries
◆ teaching staff
◆ researchers.

Students meanwhile are a more difficult category and very few institutions currently offer copyright training specifically for students, although doctoral level students often do receive some training. In the future this may become more common but in general it is recommended it is embedded into other information or digital literacy skills training.

Library staff

Library staff often form a more willing audience than other categories of staff when it comes to attending copyright training. Many library staff in front line services such as issue desks or enquiry points find that they deal with some form of copyright queries on a fairly regular basis. Queries are often related to users wanting to copy, either by photocopying or scanning, library-owned materials. Also, copyright issues do arise in the course of library users asking about services generally. It is important to ensure that existing staff along with all new staff are kept up to date with the latest developments in terms of copyright. For example, following the 2003 amendments to the Copyright Act, users copying for commercial purposes can no longer claim 'fair dealing'. This means that libraries now offer the facility to make commercial copies under the CLA Sticker scheme. It is also worth highlighting to staff that although the Copyright Act dates from 1988, numerous amendments have been made to the Act since this date. While many of the changes are minimal, as the law and licences change it is good practice to offer copyright refresher training. In addition some of the provisions in UK law specifically allow libraries and librarians to undertake certain unique types of copying, for example for interlibrary loan services.

Library staff working in certain areas of the library might need more intensive and focused copyright training, for example anyone preparing scanned or photocopied materials under the CLA Higher Education Licence should have a good grounding in the terms of the licence. They will undoubtedly need to consult the CLA website regularly and check lists such as excluded UK publishers and participating US and overseas publishers (CLA licences are not comprehensive, and the website lists regularly updated information about any UK publishers who have excluded some or all of their title, and any US or overseas publishers who are included in their licences). In addition, staff dealing with journals should also be familiar with the different types of journal licences and what standard clauses allow and do not permit in terms of making multiple copies of this type of content. As mentioned previously, staff dealing with interlibrary loans often need a good working knowledge of copyright, as do those who deal with special collections or archival materials. Finally another important area in libraries is digitization (either for preservation or to improve access to a collection). Digitizing material usually involves becoming familiar with copyright laws to a considerable extent, whether material is in copyright or not. Related to this are recent initiatives in the area of developing institutional repositories or research materials. Again, knowledge about copyright in this area is important as staff are making copyright materials available in the public domain.

It would be good practice to offer specific copyright sessions for library staff, so that the training can focus on the information key to their role. Sometimes this specialist knowledge can be obtained by sending staff on external training courses, but where staff need a more working knowledge, cascading this training internally can be more cost- and time-effective.

Learning support staff

Learning support staff are an increasingly important group of 'new professionals' in many educational establishments. Many organizations now employ staff with specific responsibility for e-learning or the VLE, sometimes called learning technologists, educational technologists or e-learning specialists. Educational developers are another important group who advise staff about pedagogy and good teaching practice. Most universities and increasing numbers of colleges employ staff in this area, although in schools this is less common. There are also a range of learning support staff that provide study skills advice to students and support specific groups of students such as those with disabilities. All of these groups of staff should ideally routinely receive copyright training as part of their induction process. In practice this is only more recently starting to happen, as IPR and copyright issues are becoming increasingly high profile particularly in the e-learning field.

If we turn first to staff who support and facilitate e-learning, the nature of their work, which often involves helping staff prepare e-learning materials, means that they are ideally placed to advise about copyright issues, alongside providing technical and pedagogical advice. Encouraging these staff to attend training might be met with some initial resistance as they can perceive copyright laws as being restrictive, leading them to have to tell teachers they cannot do certain things. In general, learning technologists often like to be perceived as 'enablers' who find ways to make things happen. Having to prevent teaching staff from doing something on copyright grounds may present them with an unfamiliar and uncomfortable situation. Nevertheless, it is essential that learning support staff do have some understanding of copyright, to avoid being personally implicated in any infringing activity a teacher undertakes. At LSE, all the learning technologists are familiar in the basics of copyright law. This means that they can advise staff on the best ways, both technically and legally, to put materials online. They can also rectify any problems that might arise when teaching staff are less familiar with copyright issues, such as removing journal article files from a course and showing the lecturer how to link to these resources.

Increasingly higher education institutions are expecting academic staff to undertake a formal teaching qualification such as a postgraduate diploma. While mandatory for a long time in the schools sector, teaching training is a relatively new area in higher education. It is clear that the curriculum of many teaching qualifications only looks very briefly at issues such as legal compliance and copyright issues, and there is a gap here that needs to be filled through a staff development programme.

Administrators and secretarial staff

In the education sector, administrators, department or faculty managers and secretaries are also an extremely important audience to reach in terms of copyright training. While it is now less common in universities for lecturing staff to have their own secretaries, much of the administration of teaching is still undertaken by these groups of staff who might work for a group of lecturers or a department. In the past, administrative staff prepared photocopies and paper course packs for students, whereas now they are increasingly uploading content to the virtual learning environment on behalf of lecturers. If these staff have an understanding and awareness of copyright issues then they can act as eyes and ears within a department. They can also spread good practice across their department and influence the behaviour of teachers. Conversely, if these staff do not understand or recognize the importance of copyright, then infringement is likely and teaching staff might continue to infringe copyright unaware that they are doing something wrong. It will be important that these staff understand the basics of copyright law, but also the main terms and conditions of licensing schemes such as the CLA Licence.

Teaching staff

Teaching staff including lecturers are always going to be a difficult and challenging audience, as traditionally they may well perceive copyright as a restriction that gets in the way of the education process. There are real opportunities to offer copyright training to these staff as part of their induction process. In addition, many new teaching staff are now required to attend specific training, for example, to undertake a postgraduate qualification in teaching. If copyright training is delivered in this manner, alongside issues such as health and safety for example, then it will certainly reach a wide audience. However, the problem with being obliged to attend certain training sessions is that it tends to make an audience view a subject fairly negatively. In addition, copyright training for teaching staff should ideally be reinforced over time – and staff kept up to date with the latest developments – rather than simply being covered in the induction process. However, if copyright training is delivered to learning support staff and administrative staff within their departments it can ensure that the training of teachers is more successful. Administrative staff can help to reinforce the copyright good practice principles in subsequent training or induction events aimed at teachers.

Research staff

Researchers are another important target group for copyright training, and in fact are becoming an increasingly receptive market as their need to understand a host of IPR issues has become more important recently. The development of open access repositories in many higher education institutions, for example, has raised the profile of copyright issues, as research staff start to question whether they 'must' transfer their copyright to a journal publisher and if this then means that they are not able to copy the work themselves. Support and training for researchers is a growing area of interest particularly in higher education or research institutions. Copyright training and advice therefore can slot easily into the training programmes that might be already under development. It is often appropriate to include PhD students in any copyright training aimed at researchers.

Case Study 7: Developing a copyright training programme for staff at LSE, UK

Introduction and background

The London School of Economics and Political Science (LSE) is the top ranked social sciences university in the UK. It has approximately 9000 full-time students, of which almost 50% are postgraduate students. It is a campus-based university in central London and while it does not offer distance learning courses, since 1999 it has used technology to support on-campus students. LSE staff are supported in their use of e-learning by the Centre for Learning Technology (CLT). The Centre currently employs nine members of staff, including the CLT Director, five learning technologists, a media specialist, a systems administrator and a librarian.

LSE does not have a dedicated Copyright Officer; however the Learning Technology Librarian provides advice and support to staff specifically concerning e-learning and copyright. This case study illustrates how LSE ensure that staff using technology in their teaching are aware of the copyright issues. Further information about the team is available from http://clt.lse.ac.uk.

E-learning at LSE

LSE have used Moodle as their institutional VLE since 2007, to provide online support for face-to-face teaching. Moodle is open-source software and while its use is not mandatory, teaching staff are encouraged to make reading lists and lecture material available online. In 2008 lecture capture software, *Echo360*, was installed in many of the large lecture theatres around the campus and recordings of lectures are scheduled upon request from the members of academic staff. In addition LSE Library is one of the largest libraries in the world devoted to the economic and social sciences and is extremely well resourced in terms of access to over 30,000 e-journals and extensive e-book collections. The Library has operated a scanning service for core readings since 1999, known as the 'electronic course pack service,' and a dedicated team check licences and obtain copyright permissions.

Documentation and guides

The Centre for Learning Technology has a considerable amount of information about copyright and e-learning available on their website. This can be viewed at: http://clt.lse.ac.uk/Copyright/index.php.

This information is aimed at academic and administrative staff at LSE who use Moodle or other learning technologies. The site includes a frequently asked questions section along with links to the electronic course pack service, which allows staff to request core readings in scanned format under the CLA's Photocopying and Scanning Higher Education Licence. In addition to the website, two printed guides are produced and distributed to staff, including a guide entitled 'Copyright and E-learning' and a more general guide entitled an 'Introduction to Copyright for LSE staff'. These guides are given out during Moodle training sessions, at lunchtime seminars and during new academic staff inductions. They are also distributed to department managers who can pass them on to teaching staff.

Training and support

Dedicated copyright training sessions are run throughout the year and open to all staff at LSE. They are routinely advertised in the all staff newsletter and on the CLT e-mail list which is sent to all staff using Moodle. The first copyright training session is usually held in the autumn term in November or December to appeal to new staff. It is entitled 'An introduction to copyright for LSE staff'. This is followed in the spring and summer with two courses on Copyright, the internet and teaching online.

Training and support offered by the CLT also includes a session on making a reading list available in Moodle. This hands-on training session covers how to link to existing electronic resources such as e-books or e-journals, how to create links to scanned readings requested as part of the Epack service and how to link to material on the web. Copyright advice is incorporated into this training session which is held in a computer laboratory.

Other sessions run by the Centre for Learning Technology that also include copyright advice include a hands-on session about how to find and use images in teaching. Copyright advice when using images, including sources of copyright-free or licensed images, is covered in this session. A similar session on finding and using digital media also covers aspects of copyright training.

A dedicated e-mail service for copyright queries is advertised widely and copyright queries are frequently dealt with by the Learning Technology Librarian. These are received by e-mail and by telephone. A sample of the queries in a typical week might include:

◆ questions about academics' own copyright agreements and whether material they have published in books or journals can be used in e-learning
◆ queries about using images from websites
◆ advice about linking or downloading articles from a subscription database such as Westlaw
◆ advice about using a government report from the Department of Health website
◆ advice about including a digitized television broadcast in Moodle and whether this can be made available to students.

Other copyright information

At LSE copyright compliance is handled centrally by the Planning and Corporate Policy Division (PCPD), although they do not employ a dedicated Copyright Officer. PCPD manage the CLA Licence and collate information about other licences that the School holds, such as the ERA Licence. A copyright poster was developed in conjunction with the Learning Technology Librarian and this is displayed throughout the LSE by photocopiers and scanners. This reminds staff (and students) of the terms of the CLA Licence. It also informs staff that any scanning requests for teaching purposes are handled by the Library's electronic course pack service and that staff should not scan copyright works for teaching purposes themselves. Retaining central control of scanning in the Library has been an important message to convey to staff at all levels and several e-mails have been sent to department managers to remind them of this.

The Reprographics department at LSE also work with CLT and PCPD to ensure notices are in place throughout the LSE and that all staff are notified about the electronic course pack service. They also distribute the Copyright and E-learning booklet as part of the staff training they undertake to use the photocopier-scanners.

Problems and issues

Since Moodle was rolled out widely across LSE academic departments, routine monitoring of the VLE for copyright compliance has not been feasible. Staff are expected to take responsibility for any content that they place online for students. However, if a member of CLT finds infringing materials in Moodle they will inform the Learning Technology Librarian. Further help and support will be offered to staff to find a legitimate way of providing students with access to the material. For example, copyright permission may be obtained to include the material, or in the case of an e-journal article, a stable link to the content can be added instead of the PDF file. Services such as the Epack service are widely promoted to enable staff to include scanned readings in their course under the terms of the CLA Licence. However, occasionally staff are told to remove material from their course if it is found to infringe copyright.

Lecture capture has caused additional copyright issues at LSE as some staff were unaware that showing third-party content such as video-recordings in lectures might lead to copyright infringement when this is recorded. In addition, images included in PowerPoint presentations can also be problematic when the source of the image is unclear. Further information is now available on the CLT website to remind staff using the lecture capture service that they must take care not to infringe copyright: http://clt.lse.ac.uk/Copyright/Copyright-And-Recorded-Lectures.php.

The Learning Technology Librarian will help staff obtain permission to reuse any materials such as video or audio in their online course. There are also standard permission letters that staff can use if they wish to include content from the web in their online course. The advice given tends to be risk adverse, and staff are encouraged to seek permission for any third-party material or to remove it from their teaching materials before uploading it to Moodle. They are, however, encouraged to make use of the generous terms of licences such as the CLA and ERA Licences, to utilize the wealth of digital resources that the Library subscribe to and to find and locate materials licensed under Creative Commons. While LSE's approach may seem cautious, it is partly to safeguard the reputation of LSE and to ensure that good practice is followed at all times.

Conclusion

This case study shows how copyright advice and support for e-learning can be managed in a university which does not employ a dedicated Copyright Officer. A wide variety of opportunities are available to staff to learn about copyright in the context of e-learning, although ultimately they are encouraged to take responsibility for the content in their online course. A permissions service, regular training sessions and an advice service helps ensure that staff do not upload illegal material to Moodle. In addition, CLT have recently devised Terms of Use for Moodle that require staff to abide by copyright law. In summary, copyright advice has become part of best practice in e-learning at LSE, so that the CLT encourage teaching staff to design their online courses using digital resources legally.

Face-to-face training sessions

Offering face-to-face training sessions may seem the obvious approach to providing copyright training. It is possible to deliver training to people in fairly large groups via a lecture-style presentation. However, in general, a more effective session usually includes an element of interaction and if the intention is to deal with specific queries during the session then training groups of no more than ten to fifteen staff is advisable. Sessions should be planned and advertised to staff only after considering a series of largely practical issues such as timing and location. However, as with any training session, it is important to have clear aims and objectives at the outset and learning outcomes that you want participants to be able to demonstrate on its completion. This will influence the way you approach your training. For example, very few teaching staff need to be able to quote chapter and verse from sections of the Copyright, Designs and Patents Act 1988. However, you do want them to leave a session with an understanding of what they can photocopy under their institutional CLA Licence, or when they might need to seek copyright permission to copy material on the internet. Good planning is essential and you should try to focus on several key points. It may be enough for participants to leave the session knowing that there is someone who can advise them in the future and they should think twice before they copy or scan material for anything other than their own private non-commercial study.

Topics to include

This will vary depending on your organization and the groups of staff you are training, but in general a session should take the following format:

- brief factual contextual information about copyright laws including something about why they are in place
- what can be done under the law: copying limits and the duration of copyright
- principles such as fair dealing and fair use
- any licences that the institution holds that allow copying beyond the law: CLA, ERA, NLA, and so forth
- copyright and the web: terms and conditions and websites
- practicalities of getting copyright permissions.

Scenarios are often useful to illustrate your point. For example, you could ask your group to consider the following: if a teacher wants to make 50 copies of a specific book and to put it on a website, what might the issues be? Scenarios can be used to demonstrate good practice or to stimulate discussion in small groups.

Practical issues

Scheduling sessions in terms of the time of year they are offered and the time of day they are delivered needs careful planning. It might be worth experimenting with advertising a course at different times of year to see if this affects attendance. For example, in an academic institution, offering training right at the start of the autumn term is rarely a good idea as people are bombarded with new students and heavy teaching commitments. Conversely, offering courses in the summer is often not successful as lecturers and researchers may be away from their institution. Trial and error is often the only way to find the right time at your organization. For example, lunchtime sessions (where lunch is also provided) often prove popular. Experience at LSE suggests that late spring (March–May) seems to be a popular time of year for staff development activities in a university working on a traditional three-term model. Other times of year might be more appropriate in other institutions, but in general it is best to avoid peak times. In schools it might be appropriate to include an element of copyright training as part of a staff training day.

Marketing and publicity is vital in order to ensure good attendance at your courses. It's also important to try to devise an appealing title for the session and while it may seem disingenuous, sometimes not calling a session a copyright training session is key to getting a good turn out! It is worth spending some time brainstorming names for courses and running them past a few volunteers to get feedback about the titles that sound appealing. In addition, spelling out some clear objectives of what people will learn in a session and why they need to attend are key to success. Your publicity, whether it is electronic (via e-mail or on the web), or in paper form (leaflets, posters and so forth), needs to be simple, clear and eye-catching. It often pays to employ professionals in this area.

Other more practical issues you need to consider include the location for the training session and available facilities. You need to find a room in your institution that is conveniently located but also has, for example, projection facilities, and the space and ability to move the furniture around should group discussions be required.

It is important to develop a set of resources for use during the session. This might include a presentation to illustrate your talk or it might be handouts or resources for the attendees. Further details are provided later on in this chapter about booklets and leaflets that you can produce to supplement a face-to-face training session as these are also useful to distribute during training and may provide more detail or reminders of the key issues.

Using the web

The web is an important way of making copyright information available to staff. Not only can staff access the information as and when they require it, the website demonstrates to any external bodies or organizations that you are taking copyright seriously and acts as a useful point of reference for queries. Copyright advice (with suitable disclaimers) and 'frequently asked questions' are useful to include on your website and many universities now provide copyright advice for staff on their websites. If you are looking to devise copyright web pages you should consult the list produced by the University of Loughborough (2009) which includes links to the copyright advice pages produced by many UK universities. The intended audience for university copyright pages is usually their own staff members, although some universities do provide advice specifically for their students. Many of the pages are created by either librarians or dedicated Copyright Officers, who are sometimes happy to allow you to adapt their pages for your own organization. There are many similarities between the listed sites, with many providing a brief overview of UK copyright law, a guide to what can and cannot be copied, and links to further resources. Once you have set up a simple copyright help page, it can be added to over time as queries arise. You should also consider keeping usage statistics of your website to monitor the numbers of people who are viewing this information.

If you already have copyright web pages or do not feel happy with this content being available on the internet to those outside of your organization you might want to consider using the virtual learning environment to develop an online course about copyright. The tools available in the VLE mean that you can monitor who has completed the course. You can also use assessment tools or communication tools to make the course more interactive. Figure 6.1 shows a screenshot from the online course 'Copyright, the internet and teaching online' which is available to all staff at LSE. This course compliments the face-to-face training session offered to staff throughout the year, described in more detail in Case Study 7. However, in addition to including resources from the class, such as the presentation and handouts, content is available to work through online, divided into bite-sized chunks. The materials have been divided into three sections and each section is followed by a short quiz to check the participants' understanding. The course is highlighted during the face-to-face session but has also been advertised to all staff using the weekly staff newsletter.

The course also includes links to useful external resources, such as the Copyright Licensing Agency's website and the UK Intellectual Property website.

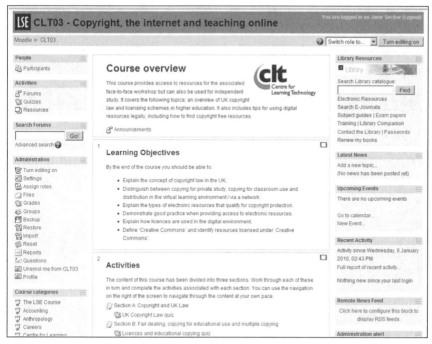

Figure 6.1 *LSE Centre for Learning Technology: Copyright, the internet and teaching online: An online course for staff*

Booklets, guides and leaflets

In the digital age the assumption might follow that more traditional help in the form of booklets and leaflets is redundant. However, personal experience at LSE suggests that teaching and administrative staff often respond positively to a hardcopy guide and seem to be more likely to refer to this, rather than to remember to read a web page. Booklets and leaflets are also another useful outward signal that you are taking copyright issues seriously to external bodies and publishers. You also don't need to have a large budget to produce such materials. They can be given to staff during training sessions, but can also be included in induction packs for new staff. A well written and concise guide has the advantage of portability over online materials, despite being less easy to keep up to date. The guide produced at LSE is designed as a 'frequently asked questions' about Copyright and E-learning. This compliments a more general guide for staff about copyright (see Figure 6.2 for a sample screenshot from the web-based

Figure 6.2 *A short guide to Copyright for LSE Staff,*
www2.lse.ac.uk/library/services/liaison/ShortGuideToCopyright.aspx

version). Both of the guides can be consulted online (LSE, 2009a; LSE, 2009b), but those wishing to see the printed booklets can contact the author for more details.

One final issue with producing written guides either in printed form, or on the web, is that you should ensure the advice you give is accurate. Therefore it may be necessary to employ an external consultant or even an IPR lawyer to oversee or proofread the guide. Printed guides also need to be kept up to date and synchronized with web-based publications that may exist to ensure that there are no discrepancies in the content.

Dealing with queries

In offering copyright training and advice you will inevitably receive a certain number of queries from staff in your organization following their attendance at a course, or from someone who might have read a leaflet or booklet but who requires further advice. It is important to consider how your organization might manage these queries and to decide:

◆ who is the best person to answer the query
◆ what to do if a query goes beyond your own understanding
◆ if queries should be managed in any way in order to keep track of the type and frequency of queries.

It can be helpful to map out who is responsible for answering specific copyright queries. Clearly if your organization is fortunate enough to have a dedicated Copyright Officer, this might be one person. However, in many organizations several people might share the knowledge, and staff may wish to get a second opinion before they offer advice to teachers.

The key issue when offering copyright advice is to be clear about the limits of your knowledge. If you are unsure of the answer, it is better to take further advice from a colleague, or to undertake further research into the issue using resources such as books or websites listed at the end of this book. Quick reference books such as Norman (2004) and Cornish (2009) are particularly useful for those in the UK as they are set out in the form of frequently asked questions. It is also worth remembering that in many copyright laws, there are grey areas. For example in the UK some terms in the Act, such as 'substantial part' are not well defined and subject to interpretation and case law. In some instances answering a copyright query may involve making a judgement based on a risk-assessment. There may be instances where providing someone with a concrete answer is difficult and while you may want to be helpful, you need to be cautious in your advice. Anyone who is charged with providing copyright advice, but who is not legally qualified, should frame his or her advice with suitable disclaimers. It is important to stress to staff looking for advice that sometimes it is down to their own judgement whether they go ahead with the activity in question.

Sources of further advice and support

Professional bodies offering copyright training courses are listed in the Conclusion. However, it is advisable that copyright trainers within an institution join a network to provide themselves with contacts and support if they are unable to answer queries from members of staff at their own organization. In the UK e-mail lists maintained by JISCmail can be important sources of advice and many Copyright Officers have joined LIS-copyseek (www.jiscmail.ac.uk/lists/lis-copyseek.html). This is a closed list open to those in the higher education community. While it does not deal specifically with e-learning but rather covers all types of copyright issues, increasingly e-learning is a feature of the queries posted here. The HERON service also maintains a closed list for their members which is operated by JISCmail. Finally JISC Legal (www.jisclegal.ac.uk) is a valuable source of advice for matters relating to copyright. As well as the guidance on their website and publications they also maintain a Helpdesk for queries.

Meanwhile in the United States the Association of Research Libraries (ARL) used to run a mailing list covering electronic reserves. This is now managed by Princeton University and is a useful source of advice for those running electronic reserves services. You will find it listed in the Conclusion.

Additional contacts are often perhaps best obtained through attending a training course and meeting individuals in other organizations undertaking similar roles.

Conclusion

This chapter examined the design and delivery of copyright training within an organization. It considered the trainer and their needs, the audience for training sessions, the format, marketing and other publicity materials. In addition the chapter has provided a case study from LSE and sources of further help and advice. While no approach is fail safe, establishing a professional and timely copyright training programme that is well supported with web-based resources, leaflets and other documentation, should go a long way to ensuring that staff within an organization are informed about copyright and follow good practice. It is also important to be realistic about your role as the trainer, whether you are formally a Copyright Officer, or if it is just one of your responsibilities. Some staff might remain resistant to attending training sessions, or following your advice. Ultimately the decision to abide by copyright laws is the responsibility of the individual. Provided you take reasonable steps to offer training at the point of need, this should offer protection for your organization.

References

Cornish, Graham (2009) *Copyright: interpreting the law for libraries, archives and information services*, 5th edn, Facet Publishing.

CLA (2009) *Copyright Licensing Agency: FAQs on compliance audits*, www.cla.co.uk/data/pdfs/he/he_audit_faqs.pdf [accessed 8 January 2010].

LSE (2009a) *Centre for Learning Technology: copyright frequently asked questions*, http://clt.lse.ac.uk/Copyright/Copyright-FAQs.php [accessed 8 January 2010].

LSE (2009b) *A Short Guide to Copyright for LSE staff*, www2.lse.ac.uk/library/services/liaison/ShortGuideToCopyright.aspx [accessed 8 Jan 2010].

Norman, S. (2004) *Practical Copyright for Information Professionals: the CILIP handbook*, Facet Publishing.

University of Loughborough (2009) *A–Z List of UK HEI Copyright Pages*, www.lboro.ac.uk/library/skills/crightpages.html [accessed 8th January 2010].

◆ Conclusion

THIS BOOK HAS considered a wide range of copyright issues associated with e-learning. It has sought to provide practical advice for those working in education and to give readers a working knowledge of copyright law as it applies in this field. It has considered the nature of the digital classroom, the different ways to support learning using an e-learning platform and why copyright is an important issue. One key advantage with online learning is that the teacher and the student can be many miles apart, even in different countries. While many institutions use e-learning to support face-to-face students, it does also offer the potential to provide education to students around the world. Yet we have seen that differences in copyright laws in different countries dictate what teachers in those countries can do, and legislation influences the way we can teach online.

Despite international copyright agreements such as the Berne Convention, copyright laws are not the same in every country, and the educational exceptions differ. Consequently, teachers in UK educational establishments must abide by UK law even if the students they teach are elsewhere in the world. In some respects copyright laws in countries such as the United States, where a teacher can claim 'fair use', are more permissive, giving them advantages in terms of the content they can distribute to students. Some educators in the UK believe that they are hampered by the minimal copyright exceptions in UK law for educational use. However there are several valuable licensing schemes that facilitate the distribution of digital content to students. Many teachers believe that copyright restrictions are counter-productive and out of step with what technology now permits. While this may be partly true, this book provides advice and guidance to help institutions stay within the law. Copyright is an issue that educational establishments around the world need to consider as technology has facilitated the unprecedented sharing of digital content. This book urges institutions to take copyright issues seriously. They should seek to embed copyright and IPR policies into their teaching strategies, to ensure staff (and students) are not infringing the rights of others in a bid to make content available. There is much that can be done under the current legislative framework in the UK, and ensuring that staff have a good understanding of copyright before they use e-learning will avoid many difficulties. The key advice is to consider copyright issues at the outset of an e-learning venture and to design e-learning with an awareness of what copyright laws and licences allow.

The book has considered the issues associated with the digitization of print-based resources and the reuse of existing digital content. It has looked at text, images and multimedia. It has also considered emerging technologies, tools and services or Web 2.0 technologies. Finally it provided advice on how to establish a rigorous copyright training programme within an institution. However, no book on this topic can hope to answer every question that the reader might have. In addition, educational technology is developing rapidly, giving rise to new scenarios and new copyright challenges. Around the world countries are seeking to respond to technological developments and to adapt and modify their copyright laws. The section below therefore provides some useful resources for keeping up to date in this area. The resources are organized by topic broadly related to each of the chapters of this book, although some specific country-related resources are also included. The listing includes books, websites, blogs and mailing lists that should provide useful sources of further advice, training and support.

Organizations in the education sector occasionally organize one-off events on copyright and e-learning which tend to be widely publicized. It is useful to subscribe to various mailing lists and blogs to keep up to date in this field and a selection are listed below. A list of useful copyright resources is also maintained in Delicious at: http://delicious.com/lse_lassie/copyright.

 **Further resources**

General resources on copyright

Mailing lists

Center for Intellectual Property (2009) Digital Copyright: electronic
mailing list,
www.umuc.edu/distance/odell/cip/listserv.shtml#digital.

JISC-DRM (2009) *JISC Digital Rights Management Discussion List*,
JISC-DRM@JISCMAIL.AC.UK.

Library E-reserves discussion list, LIB-ERESERVES@PRINCETON.EDU,
http://library.princeton.edu/services/listserv.php.

LIS-Copyseek (2009) *JISCMAIL Closed Discussion List for Copyright
Queries*,
LIS-Copyseek@jiscmail.ac.uk .

Copyright law resources by country

UK

CILIP Library and Archives Copyright Alliance,
www.cilip.org.uk/get-
involved/advocacy/copyright/pages/about.aspx.

Cornish, G. (2009) *Copyright: interpreting the law for libraries, archives and
information services*, 5th edn, Facet Publishing.

Norman, S. (2004) *Practical Copyright for Information Professionals: the
CILIP handbook*, Facet Publishing.

Pedley, P. (2005) *Managing Digital Rights: a practitioner's guide*, Facet
 Publishing.
Pedley, P. (2007) *Digital Copyright*, Facet Publishing.
Pedley, P. (2008) *Copyright Compliance: practical steps to stay within the law*,
 Facet Publishing.
UK Intellectual Property Office,
 www.ipo.gov.uk/home.htm.

International

World Intellectual Property Organization,
 www.wipo.org.int.
World Intellectual Property Organization (2009) *Collection of Laws for
 Electronic Access (CLEA)*,
 www.wipo.int/clea/en.
 This database provides access to intellectual property legislation
 from a wide range of countries and regions as well as to treaties on
 intellectual property.

Europe

The Copyright Association of Ireland,
 www.cai.ie/index.htm.
European Digital Rights,
 www.edri.org.
 An organization set up to defend civil rights in the information
 society and foster cooperation in Europe regarding the internet,
 copyright and privacy issues.

Canada

Association of Universities and Colleges of Canada Statement on copyright,
 www.aucc.ca/policy/issues/copyright_e.html.
Canadian Library Association (2008) *Copyright Information*,
 www.cla.ca/AM/Template.cfm?Section=Copyright_Information.

Murray, L. J. (2009) *Fair Copyright*,
   www.faircopyright.ca.

New Zealand and Australia

Australian Copyright Council,
   www.copyright.org.au.
The Copyright Council of New Zealand,
   www.copyright.org.nz.
IP Australia – Australian Government,
   www.ipaustralia.gov.au/ip/copyright.shtml.
The Library and Information Association of New Zealand Aotearoa
   (LIANZA), *New Zealand publications on copyright of interest to
   librarians*,
   www.lianza.org.nz/publications/copyright.html.

United States of America

Association of Research Libraries (2009) *Know your Copy Rights: using
   copyright works in academic settings*,
   www.knowyourcopyrights.org.
Barach College/CUNY (2009) *Interactive Guide to using Copyrighted Media
   in your Courses*,
   www.baruch.cuny.edu/tutorials/copyright.
Brewer, M. (2008) *Fair Use Evaluator*, ALA Office for Information
   Technology Policy,
   http://librarycopyright.net/fairuse.
Columbia University Libraries/Information Services (2009) *Copyright
   Advisory Office*,
   http://copyright.columbia.edu/copyright/.
Copyright Clearance Center,
   www.copyright.com.
   US Reprographic Rights organization offering licensing and
   permissions to copying beyond statutory limits. Also provide advice
   and training.
Harris, L. E. (2002) *Licensing Digital Content: a practical guide for librarians*,
   ALA Editions.

Library Copyright Alliance,
   www.librarycopyrightalliance.org.
Library Law Blog (2009),
   http://blog.librarylaw.com.
Strong, W. S. (1999) *The Copyright Book: a practical guide*, 5th edn.,
   MIT Press.
United States Copyright Office,
   www.copyright.gov.

Further reading on e-learning

There are numerous resources specifically focusing on e-learning, learning technologies and classroom technologies, including monographs and journals. Those wishing to get a general overview of this topic are advised to consult the websites detailed below.

Association of Learning Technology (ALT): www.alt.ac.uk

The Association of Learning Technology is the UK's professional and scholarly body for those with an interest in the use of learning technology. It publishes a journal and newsletter, and an annual conference and other events.

Becta: www.becta.org.uk

Becta is the government agency for effective use of technology in education, particularly aimed at the school, further education and lifelong learning sector.

EDUCAUSE: www.educause.edu

EDUCAUSE is a US not-for-profit organization that aims 'to advance higher education through the intelligent use of information technology'. It provides advice, resources and publications in a variety of areas including copyright, but also advice on using digital media and lecture capture. The resources can be browsed or searched.

E-learning Network of Australasia: www.elnet.com.au

An Australian membership organization for e-learning professionals in business and education. It organizes events, provides a news service, has a range of resources related to e-learning on its website and publishes an online journal.

Joint Information Systems Committee (JISC): www.jisc.ac.uk

Funded by the UK HE and FE funding bodies to provide world-class leadership in the innovative use of ICT to support education and research, JISC manage and fund a range of projects and services for the HE and FE community around eight strategic themes including e-learning. It organizes events and training, and provides news, resources and publications from this extensive website.

Copyright and e-learning

Agnew, G. (2008) *Digital Rights Management: a librarian's guide to technology and practise*, Chandos Publishing.
Casey, J. (2006) *Getting Practical with IPR in E-Learning*, http://trustdr.ulster.ac.uk/outputs/gettingPracticalWithIPR.php.
Eduserv (2007) *Copyright Toolkit*, http://copyrighttoolkit.com/index.html.
HEFCE (2006) *Intellectual Property Rights in e-Learning Programmes, Guidance for senior managers*, www.hefce.ac.uk/pubs/hefce/2006/06_20.
JISC (2006) *Intellectual Property Rights (IPR) in Networked E-Learning*, www.jisclegal.ac.uk/ManageContent/ViewDetail/tabid/243/ID/130/Intellectual-Property-Rights-IPR-in-Networked-E-Learning—28042006.aspx.
JISCLegal (2006, 22 March) *Copyright and eLearning: Webcast*, www.jisclegal.ac.uk/ManageContent/ViewDetail/tabid/243/ID/93/Webcast—Copyright-e-Learning—22032006.aspx.
Secker, J. (2004) *Electronic Resources in the Virtual Learning Environment*, Chandos Publishing.
Strategic Content Alliance/JISC (2009) *IPR Toolkit* http://sca.jiscinvolve.org/files/2009/10/sca_ipr_toolkit-v2-01_intro.pdf.

Web 2.0 and copyright

Australian Copyright Council (2009) *User Generated Content and Web 2.0 Websites*, Information Sheet: G108v01,
www.copyright.org.au/g108.pdf.

Cornish, G. (2009) *Copyright: interpreting the law for libraries, archives and information services*, 5th edn, Facet Publishing, 164–6.

JISC (2008) *Web 2.0 and Intellectual Property Rights*,
www.jisc.ac.uk/publications/documents/bpweb20iprv1.aspx.

JISC (2009) *Web2Rights*,
www.web2rights.org.uk/Toolkit;
www.web2rights.org.uk/documents.html.

JISCLegal (2008) *Web 2.0 Legal Toolkit*,
www.jisclegal.ac.uk/ManageContent/ViewDetail/tabid/243/ID/895/Web-20-Legal-Toolkit—30102008.aspx.

JISCLegal (2009) *Web 2.0 and Legal Issues*,
www.jisclegal.ac.uk/Themes/Web20.aspx.

Copyright and multimedia

Aside from the relevant reprographic organizations there are several specialist organizations offering advice for those specifically interested in using multimedia content in e-learning. The following is just a selection of these organizations and does not constitute a comprehensive list:

American Library Association Factsheet on Copyright and Video: www.ala.org/ala/aboutala/offices/library/libraryfactsheet/alalibraryfactsheet7.cfm

Produced by the American Library Association this is a useful online guide to copyright and multimedia (largely video resources) in the United States. Last updated in August 2009 it includes links to various sources of additional advice and support.

British Universities Film and Video Council: http://bufvc.ac.uk

A useful source of advice, training and support largely aimed at those in the education sector in the UK. BUFVC is a membership organization and members include higher and further education institutions, schools, specialist institutes, commercial companies and broadcasters.

Copyright Issues: Multimedia and internet resources: www.utsystem.edu/ogc/intellectualproperty/mmfruse.htm

This resource has been produced by Georgia W. Harper, the Scholary Communications Advisor at the University of Texas and is part of a wider Crash Course in Copyright. The resource is licensed under a Creative Commons License and provides specific copyright advice for using multimedia content covering topics such as fair use, digitizing content and managing permissions. This is particularly useful for those working in higher education in the United States.

Frankel, J. T. (2009) *Teacher's Guide to Music: media and copyright law*,
Music Pro Guides.

JISC Digital Media: www.jiscdigitalmedia.ac.uk

JISC Digital Media is a source of advice, training and support for those working in higher and further education in the UK. Formerly known as TASI (Technical Advisory Service for Images), this organization was expanded to cover all types of digital media including images, moving images and sound recordings: www.jiscdigitalmedia.ac.uk.

Movie Licensing USA: www.movlic.com

Movie Licensing USA offers licences to K-12 schools and public libraries to allow them to legally show movies for entertainment (as opposed to teaching) purposes. An annual site licence can be purchased, or a one-off licence. Site includes information about the education exemption under US copyright law and when this applies.

SURFmedia: www.surfmedia.nl/index.html

SURF are the Dutch equivalent of JISC and they have a website providing advice and support to those in education dealing with multimedia.

Smartcopying: www.smartcopying.edu.au

Smartcopying provides advice for schools in Australia on all aspects of copyright, including details about format shifting and multimedia copying of film, video and DVDs and musical works. The website is produced by a committee of the Australian Ministerial Council on Education, Employment, Training and Youth Affairs (MCEETYA).

Sample of university IPR policies

Columbia University (2000) *Columbia University Copyright Policy*,
    www.columbia.edu/cu/provost/docs/copyright.html [accessed 13
    February 2010]
MIT (n.d.) *MIT Policies & Procedures*,
    http://web.mit.edu/policies/13/13.1.html [accessed 13 February 2010].
University of Cambridge *Intellectual Property Rights*,
    www.enterprise.cam.ac.uk/uploads/File/Inventions_IP_Licensing/IP
    RCouncilsRevOrdinance27Jul2005Voted12DecJul2006.pdf [accessed
    13 February 2010].
UCL (2009) *UCL Staff IPR Policy*
    www.ucl.ac.uk/Library/scholarly-communication/ipr.shtml [accessed
    13 February 2010].
University of Otago (2009) *Intellectual Property Rights Policy*
    www.otagouniversity.co.nz/administration/policies/otago003229.htm
    l [accessed 13 February 2010].
Queensland University of Technology (2008) *Intellectual Property Policy*,
    www.mopp.qut.edu.au/D/D_03_01.jsp [accessed 13 February 2010].

Sources of further copyright training

A number of organizations offer copyright training and below is a list of training providers, largely from the UK, who offer courses and events related to copyright.

Aslib Training,
    www.aslib.co.uk/training/index.htm.
Association of Learned and Professional Society Publishers (ALPSP),
    www.alpsp.org/ngen_public.

Association of Learning Technology,
     www.alt.ac.uk/events.php.
Australian Copyright Council,
     www.copyright.org.au/training.
Becta,
     www.becta.org.uk.
British Universities Film and Video Council (BUFVC),
     http://bufvc.ac.uk/courses.
Center for Intellectual Property, University of Maryland University
     College,
     www.umuc.edu/distance/odell/cip/cip.shtml.
CILIP (Chartered Institute of Library and Information Professionals),
     www.cilip.org.uk.
Copyright Circle,
     www.copyrightcircle.co.uk.
JISC Digital Media,
     www.jiscdigitalmedia.ac.uk.
TFPL,
     www.tfpl.com/training/index.cfm.

Glossary

ACRL	Association of College and Research Libraries
ALA	American Library Association
ALPSP	Association of Learned and Professional Society Publishers
ARL	Association of Research Libraries
AUCC	Association of Universities and Colleges of Canada
BUFVC	British Universities Film & Video Council
CAL	Copyright Agency Limited (Australian reprographic rights organization)
CC	Creative Commons
CCC	Copyright Clearance Center (US reprographic rights organization)
CILIP	Chartered Institute of Library and Information Professionals
CLA	Copyright Licensing Agency (UK reprographic rights organization)
CLARCS	Copyright Licensing Agency Rapid Clearance Service
CLL	Copyright Licensing Limited
CMS	course management system
CPD	continuing professional development
CONFU	Conference on Fair Use
DACS	Design and Artists Copyright Society
DCLG	Department of Communities and Local Government
DCMA	Digital Millennium Copyright Act
DCMS	Department of Culture Media and Sport

DOI	Digital Object Identifier
DRM	digital rights management
DVD	Digital Versatile Disc
EEA	European Economic Area
ECM	Electronic Course Materials
ERA	Educational Recording Agency
EU	European Union
HEI	higher education institution
HERON	Higher Education Resources ON-demand
HESS	Higher Education Scanning Service
HTML	Hypertext Markup Language
ICLA	Irish Copyright Licensing Agency
ICT	information and communication technologies
IPR	intellectual property rights
ISP	internet service provider
JANET	The network dedicated to the needs of education and research in the UK, it connects the UK's education and research organizationsto each other, as well as to the rest of the world through links to the global internet.
JISC	Joint Information Systems Committee
LACA	Library and Archives Copyright Alliance
LIANZA	Library and Information Association of New Zealand Aotearoa
LMS	learning management system
LORN	learning object repository
MERLOT	Multimedia Educational Resource for Learning and Online Teaching
NESLI	National Electronic Site Licence Initiative
NLA	Newspaper Licensing Agency
NPO	not-for-profit organization
OA	open access
OCR	optical character recognition
OECD	the Organisation for Economic Co-operation and Development
OER	open educational resources
Ofcom	Office of Communications
OGC	Office of General Counsel

OU	Open University
PDF	Portable Document File
RSS	Really Simple Syndication (see BBC definition, http://news.bbc.co.uk/1/hi/help/3223484.stm)
SCONUL	Society of College, National and University Libraries
TASI	Technical Advisory Service for Images
TLSS	The Teaching & Learning Support Section
TRILT	Television and Radio Index for Learning and Teaching
UNESCO	the United Nations Educational, Scientific and Cultural Organization
URL	Universal Resource Locator
USB	Universal Serial Bus
UUK	Universities UK
VHS	Video Home System
VIP	visually impaired person
VLE	virtual learning environment

Index